MW01223593

Curiosity's Destinations

Tales & Insights from the Life of a Geologist

Curiosity's Destinations

Tales & Insights from the Life of a Geologist

Donald McIvor

Grindstone Press
Los Angeles

Cataloguing-in-Publication Data on file with the Library of Congress

ISBN: 9745179-2-5
Published in the United States by
Grindstone Press
A Witty Fools Company
P.O. Box 481058
Los Angeles, California 90048

Curiosity's Destinations

Tales & Insights from the Life of a Geologist

Contents **Page**

Note: Parenthetic numbers, such as (4), in the text refer to sources cited in the bibliography

Foreword

Having spent forty-six of my seventy-six years being fully employed (and several more years employed part-time), I have found it interesting to observe the attitude of others toward work. I suspect that for the great majority, work provides interest and challenge, but is basically something that is required to make a living. I have known a few who never seem happy with work. Then there are the lucky few for whom it supplies lifelong fascination and enjoyment.

I belong with that lucky few. I worked for all forty-three years of my primary career with one company, and only rarely did I not enjoy it, be challenged by it, and feel fulfilled by it. My career allowed me to see many countries on every continent except Antarctica. I was able to work at a series of tasks from entry-level earth scientist to director and senior vice president of my company.

That company was Exxon, now ExxonMobil, and then as now the world's largest and demonstrably the most successful publicly owned oil company.

As noted, my work content varied enormously over time, and I got to know and relate to a large number of people in many environments, at all levels in the socioeconomic scale, and at all levels of authority from menial labor to heads of state.

This book is not about Exxon. It is not about the oil business, nor is it about earth science, except as these provided me with the means to gain insights into the world around me and to have many experiences that were of more than normal interest and sometimes even adventurous.

So, the book takes the form of a series of tales that describe these insights and experiences. It is not autobiographical except to the degree necessary to establish a context for the tales.

When I had completed some early drafts of this book and sought the opinions of friends, family, and people with knowledge of writing and publishing, the advice was centered on a common theme. It can be paraphrased like this: "You had an opportunity given to very few. You saw a great deal of the planet and its people. And considering the time span covered by your career, you saw a world that is forever changed. So don't just tell about the people and the places that you saw. Tell us what you thought about them and, above all, how they made you feel." I considered that good advice and I have tried to honor it.

And that is what follows: stories of people, places, and issues; what I thought about them, and how they made me feel. They begin with growing up on the Canadian prairie in the 1930's and end with living in a small New England town today. Between those bookends are stories of interesting and often remote places, of issues that affect people's lives, and of personal life experiences. This book describes them through the eyes and consciousness of an individual whose curiosity drove him to try to figure them out and whose storytelling genes have made him tell them.

Who am I?

My birthplace and home for the first twenty-two years of life was Winnipeg, Manitoba. It is almost dead-center on the North American continent, roughly equidistant from the Atlantic, Pacific and Arctic Oceans and the Gulf of Mexico. Being landlocked and about fifty degrees north latitude, it is a very cold place in winter (often minus forty degrees Fahrenheit) and a very hot place in summer (sometimes one hundred degrees Fahrenheit). Trees are scarce. The prairie is so remarkably flat that any hill over fifty feet has a name.

In my youth, even the original European settlers (Scots in the early Nineteenth Century) had not been there long, and much of the population consisted of Central European people even more recently come to Canada. A large fraction of my schoolmates had parents who had emigrated from the Ukraine. And the area around Winnipeg had some fascination for Icelanders, because legend had it that there were more Icelanders around Winnipeg than there were in Iceland. Across the Red River of the North lay the French Canadian city of St. Boniface.

The city's economy was based on the grain trade, and the fact that Winnipeg was the jumping off point for the metal mines in the rugged and rocky Precambrian Shield that makes up the northern two-thirds of the province. The city's motto, "Commerce, Prudence, Industry," reflects the sober view of the original Scottish settlers. The provincial logo, the North American bison, reflects the prairie environment.

What sort of family did I have? I lived with a large extended family consisting of paternal grandparents, mother, father, a sister who joined us when I was eleven, and a variety of my father's siblings depending on the availability of work in the "dirty thirties."

In the socioeconomic scale, we were lower-middle class, but what made our home remarkable was the degree to which we hewed to the Scottish tradition of stressing literacy and education. Our house had a great store of books and quality periodicals because the centerpiece in our value system was that education and literacy were the keys to "making something of oneself." This quote from Arthur Hermann's 2001 book, *How the Scots Invented the Modern World* (5), described our home situation quite accurately:

"An official national survey in 1795 showed that out of a total population of 1.5 million, nearly 20,000 Scots depended for their livelihood on writing and publishing, and 10,500 on teaching. All this meant that despite its relative poverty and small population, Scottish culture had a built-in bias toward reading, learning and education in general. In no other European country did education count for so much or enjoy such a broad base."

Having such a home environment certainly gave me a leg up in elementary and high school. Literature and language education was easy for me because of my home situation, but it was science that set me afire with a desire to know more and more, and my home situation gave me no leg up there. Mathematics and science fascinated me because they made sense of so many things that were puzzling in the world around me.

I don't actually remember this, but my truthful mother told me that when I was a preschool-age child, my nickname in my family was "Donny Why" because I taxed the patience of my relatives with questions.

So, even elementary science elated me. It may be boring to those who don't share the same interests, but seeing the reasons for natural phenomena is thrilling for those whose curiosity makes them ask "Why?"

For instance, any child living north or south of the tropics knows that below a given temperature, water becomes ice. But one's thinking and feeling about this metamorphosis alters when one understands that at thirty-two degrees Fahrenheit, the loss of latent heat reaches a point where the intermolecular forces strengthen to the degree that the liquid becomes a solid. A mental picture forms of bonds between molecules pulling tighter until they are locked together in such a way that they lose their fluidity.

There is also something very intriguing about being able to go beyond rote memorization to recognition of observable truth, or being able to represent natural phenomena by the abstractions of science and mathematics.

For instance, I was fascinated when I first became aware that the simplest of all geometric forms, a straight line, can be represented in abstract fashion by just four symbols in the equation y=mx+b where the meaning of y, m, x, and b becomes clear when the line is plotted on a chart. Or to see through the conception that arranging the elements in Mendeleev's Periodic Table allows understanding that there is a recurring pattern to the properties of the elements when they are arranged in the order of their atomic number.

When I was eleven, my life altered significantly. World War II began in September 1939. My father enlisted immediately in the Canadian Army and departed for Europe in December of that year. Modest as our circumstances had been, they became less than modest with that event. We scraped through the six war years. Two of the upcoming tales, "Learning From Two Cultures" and "A Seventeen Year Old Learns the Reality of Work" deal with events in my life triggered by WWII. The first tells of kindness from the family of an Italian-Canadian related to us by marriage; the second tells of how I managed to get started on a university education. Yet another tale, "Educating an Earth Scientist," tells something about my college experience and a lot more about some things I learned during work periods between college years.

Once graduated from college, I began what would become a forty-three-year career, first with Exxon's Canadian affiliate (Imperial Oil Limited) and later with other Exxon affiliates and with the parent company.

Most, but not all of the upcoming tales, will deal with events made possible by that career. However, because I want the main theme of this book to center around these tales rather than be autobiographical, I will now relate the course of that career in shorthand fashion as follows.

My first twelve years on the job were spent in purely technical positions in Imperial's oil and gas exploration function, with an eighteen-month break at an Exxon research facility in Tulsa, Oklahoma, and relatively short work assignments in Angola and in France.

After these purely technical endeavors, I unwillingly took my first executive job as manager of Imperial's exploration research function, an experience related in an upcoming tale titled "A Reluctant Executive." Next I became manager of Imperial's Corporate Planning Department at the company's headquarters in Toronto, much to my surprise and everyone else's. From there I went to being the company's exploration manager, got dragooned into the Canadian Armed Services for a year to be an energy expert at The National Defense College, then became a director and senior vice president of Imperial Oil Limited with responsibility for oil and gas exploration and production. At age forty-nine I assumed the same responsibilities but now for Exxon Corporation as vice president for oil and gas exploration and production at the Manhattan headquarters.

I returned to Imperial at age fifty-three to become CEO and Board Chairman of Imperial for four years. During this period I became a director of the Royal Bank of Canada.

The final eight years of my primary career were spent as director and senior vice president of Exxon Corporation with responsibility for oil and gas exploration and production, coal, minerals, Exxon Research and Engineering, and Exxon Production Research Company, first in Manhattan and then in Dallas after the corporate headquarters moved there. So it was from Dallas that I retired from my primary career at age sixty-five and moved back to the house I had kept in New Canaan, Connecticut.

Since that time I have occupied myself with a variety of endeavors that are described in a tale titled "Second Act."

That bare outline is sufficient information for readers to have a context in which they can place the following tales, which are the prime focus of this book.

Learning from Two cultures

In my formative years, most people around my home in Winnipeg still retained strong influences of the countries from which they or their parents came. What is known in Canada as The Cultural Mosaic (and in The United States as The Melting Pot) hadn't yet had time to Canadianize much of the population, particularly in Western Canada which was my home.

My family's value system came largely from Britain, particularly from the north of Scotland. As noted previously, our world view was captured in the notion that education was the key to a good place in the work force, and that if such a place were found, then all other aspects of life would likely fall into place. This was obviously an oversimplified, perhaps even naïve view, but it was actually not too bad an ethic for the time and for our situation. We had never had the luxury of forming a more sophisticated view.

My family was somewhat dour in outlook. And they were certainly not among the world's great cooks.

Again as already noted, when I was eleven, my father departed for Europe and WWII, leaving my mother, his son (me), his newborn daughter, and his mother to live on a Canadian Army enlisted man's pay for the war years 1939 to 1945.

My mother's sister had married an Italian immigrant's son, Michael Del Begio, and had a son and a daughter and a large extended Italian-Canadian family consisting of Uncle Mike's father and mother, and his sister and three brothers and their spouses and children, probably twenty people in all. Uncle Mike and the other Del Begios lived within a mile of us.

I have since deduced that on my father's departure, Uncle Mike realized that my family would be in for difficult times, and he and my aunt Emily began to include us periodically for meals with them and for gatherings of the extended Del Begio clan.

Thus began an eleven-year period in my life (until I graduated from college) when I had a relationship with Uncle Mike, Aunt Emily, my cousins and the extended Del Begio family.

As much as I loved my immediate family, I warmed to the Del Begio clan. At first they surprised me by how different they were from my family, and then they became a source of enjoyment for the same reason.

This happened in many ways. Whereas we were stoic in the face of adversity and felt it proper to deflect any compliment with, "It was nothing, really," the Del Begios gave vent to loud emotion at every turn, tore their hair in agony when things went wrong, and strutted like peacocks when good fortune came to visit. My background made me feel this was somewhat inappropriate behavior, but as time passed, I grew to relish their handling of life events. I found myself agonizing and laughing with them. They seemed to know something about enjoying being alive that had escaped my family.

And the food! Up until then I had no idea that food could be so good. There was always salad with lunch and dinner. I grew to be very fond of the spicy sauces for pasta, the veal, and the wonderful deserts. Aunt Emily was recognized by the extended Italian-Canadian family as being a great cook. Grandpa Del Begio made fine dandelion salad and dandelion wine from the spring and early summer greens and blooms.

The closeness among all members of the family appealed to me and was missing in my own family. Uncle Mike's three brothers owned a family business, and although Uncle Mike was not an active participant, he seemed to know the business as well as his brothers. Discussions of the business took place on Sundays when the clan met at one of the houses for dinner. After the meal, the men sat around the kitchen table and talked. I liked to sit off to one side and listen. Uncle Mike would try to make me feel included by saying something to me every now and then. Meanwhile, the women gathered in the living room to talk about family matters.

Uncle Mike followed my progress at school almost as closely as my mother did. In his way he was a scholarly man who got a civil engineering degree at night school at the age of fifty-two. He seemed to like my own scholarly ways, and he taught me many valuable life skills, particularly how to get along with other people. He taught me lessons that have been of great use throughout my life. One is to listen carefully to see whether someone's conversation has something to offer, and if it does, to seek to understand it through comments and questions. The second was a companion piece to the first, and that is to realize that most loud-mouth know-it-alls are hollow and full of bluster and that their facades are often easily punctured by skilled words and that if the condition persists and becomes threatening, that a swift punch in the nose often works wonders. (As the infirmities of age have crept over me, I have ceased this tactic.)

When I entered college, Uncle Mike was very proud of me and, even though my father had returned by then, he followed my studies closely. Because he was such a skilled "people person," I think Uncle Mike recognized that he could still be a father figure for me.

All told, having the Del Begio family take a significant part in my formative years was a very positive factor. At first they offered some degree of security during an insecure time. The relationship then grew into one where I learned something very important: there are ways to live other than what my immediate family practiced. My relationship with the Del Begios taught me life can be more joyful than I might have otherwise realized, and that giving vent to emotion is acceptable.

An event of global significance, World War II, set in motion a series of happenings that enriched my life.

A Seventeen-Year-old Learns the Reality of Work

If you are older than seventeen, try to think back to what it's like to be that age. I can remember, even at age seventy-six. I was physically immature, six feet tall and 150 pounds, very skinny. I had intellectual self-confidence, but like most seventeen-year-olds I was pretty insecure emotionally. I still had vast amounts to learn about the world around me.

During the summer of 2003, I began to read Anton Chekhov's short stories. In the foreword of *The Undiscovered Chekhov...Forty-Three New Stories*, (2), Peter Constantine writes, "Chekhov was the grandson of a serf. His father had run a ramshackle grocery store in Taganog in Southern Russia. When Chekhov was sixteen his father went bankrupt and left town in a hurry. He took the whole family, including his eldest sons, with him to Moscow, everyone, that is, except for young Anton, who was left destitute and penniless to fend for himself in Taganog." Years later, Chekhov wrote, "I did not have a childhood."

I feel empathy for Chekhov, even if my situation was not nearly as drastic as his. When my father left for WWII, my family had to exist on a bare minimum income for the years 1939 to 1945.

My mother was very strong and we quickly adapted. I was given to understand that I now had to become part of the family support system. For instance, we had a large vegetable garden which was a significant source of food, and this became my responsibility. So was the care of the basement coal and wood furnace in winter. If it wasn't stoked first thing in the morning and before going to bed at night, four people got pretty uncomfortable. And I learned that part-time jobs for me would be a significant part of the family cash flow.

Thus between the ages of eleven and seventeen, I had a long string of minor jobs; paper boy, delivering for a grocery store and a drug store, starter on a golf course, driving a horse-drawn delivery van on Saturdays when a nationwide department store brought these out of mothballs as a gasoline-saving patriotic gesture, and several more.

In my last year of high school, I learned that I had been awarded a scholarship to the University of Manitoba for my marks in physics and chemistry. This created conflicting feelings. My extended family and particularly my mother had convinced me that education is the key to a better life. Thus I was thrilled to be given recognition that I was capable of a university education. On the other hand, even though I desperately wanted to attend university, I couldn't see where the funds would come from. My father had just returned from WWII, and he was in no position to be of financial assistance. The type of after-school and weekend jobs I'd held would never accumulate the money required to get started. I needed some serious money and couldn't see where I was going to get it.

The scholarship was a vote of confidence in my ability, but the yawning abyss between me and the money I needed seemed an insuperable problem. But the desire to get it gave me tremendous motivation. How I managed makes an interesting tale.

What would turn out to be the answer lay in the fact that I had heard that there was "real money" to be made working in the underground metal mines of the northern part of the province. Most males between eighteen and forty were still away fighting WWII, creating a significant labor shortage in Canada. The shortage was acute in the metal mines, since this was hard, dirty work, and, although I did not yet appreciate it, dangerous work.

A few inquiries established that getting hired to work in the mines was frighteningly easy. That is how it came to pass that a short time after high school graduation, I was signed up as a miner's apprentice at some place called San Antonio Gold Mines. At seventeen I was slightly younger than five other "real money" seekers on a bus from Winnipeg to the hamlet of Lac du Bonnet, Manitoba, a float-plane base for flights into the northern wilderness.

As we got off the bus I examined the only aircraft tied up at the dock, obviously our transportation to the mine. I would learn later that it was a pre-WWII German Junkers, distinguishable by its corrugated aluminum fuselage. The pilot, a middle-aged man in dirty white coveralls, nodded to acknowledge our presence as he busied himself with his aircraft. He and the

Junkers shared something: they both looked grimy and beaten-up.

There were no seats on the plane. When we boarded, we found places on or among the cargo. We were then introduced to a fragment of aeronautical arcana. Takeoff and landing can be difficult in a float plane and it is important that the load be as far forward as possible. Because we were not strapped down to seats, we were requested to huddle at the front of the cabin until we were well aloft.

The cabin stank from years of spilled gasoline. We never climbed above a few thousand feet, so we felt the full effect of the bumps and lurches caused by the hot June thermals. The gasoline stench and the bumps made first one and then, naturally, all passengers airsick. I have a strong nauseous memory of being sick in my own hat. The pilot seemed totally calm about six airsick passengers. Since I had never flown before, I probably concluded that getting sick is an everyday part of air-travel.

In about three hours, we saw a collection of buildings along the shore of a lake. Their function puzzled me. Soon I learned I had seen my first gold mine.

It was obvious that the six gray-faced individuals who stumbled off the Junkers did not impress the one-man welcoming committee. This was not hard to understand. No doubt he had grown used to making do with whatever help showed up. He instructed us where to bunk, where to eat, where to get work-clothes, where to show up for work next morning.

At our first meal at the mess hall, we learned a new fact: there was no conversation while eating. Meals, which were very good, were a refueling operation to be completed with dispatch.

Next morning when we showed up at the change-house, we learned something else. The room in which we changed into work gear filled with a gray cloud without any explanation. We were later told that the gray cloud was powdered aluminum, which was thought to prevent silicosis.

We were issued hard hats, belts with an attached battery on them, and lamps that hooked to the hard hat and the battery. Thus equipped, I was told that I would be a "grizzly man" on a "tramming crew," phrases that meant nothing to me. An inquiry as to what all this meant was met with a terse "you'll see." Indoctrination was not a big item here. Or maybe it was. Read on.

The recruits got into "the cage" (read "elevator"). I was let off at "the level" where I would be working, about 2500 feet below surface.

The atmosphere was cold and damp. A few bulbs lit the immediate area, but beyond that was total blackness. I could hear jackhammers in the distance, and every now and then an explosion.

The crew that I tagged up with was a rough looking lot, not exactly Oxford Dons. The man who proved to be the crew leader (there were no rank badges) greeted me and led me to an excavation off to one side of the mine shaft I had just exited. It was about twenty feet by twenty feet in area and about six feet deep. Its floor was formed by a grid of railway rails spaced so that one square-foot holes separated them. This was the "grizzly".

Ore trains drew up to the grizzly and dumped their cargo onto the rails. My job, it was explained, would be to take a twelve-pound sledgehammer and persuade the ore to go through the one square-foot holes so it could be hauled up the mineshaft to the surface in a huge bucket. Some of the ore-chunks were as big as refrigerators.

I was not elated at the prospect, but a commitment had been made, so I set to work with a will. However, some big rocks took a lot of sledgehammer blows without much result. In what seemed no time at all, another trainload of ore arrived with individuals who looked with silent disapproval at my lack of progress. Their opinion was obviously that my performance was sub-par.

It needs explanation that during that era, Canadian mines operated on what was called "the bonus system." Wages were pitifully small, and "the real money" I had come to seek lay in bonus payments based on the amount of ore that a crew, working as a team, blasted loose from the earth, hauled in trains (hence "tramming") and sent on its way to surface. In this situation my performance was a bottleneck on the earning power of the entire crew. Lest the significance of this fact might escape my understanding, it was explained very forcefully.

The leader offered a solution. If I could not keep up by using the sledgehammer, I would need to use dynamite on the big chunks. At this I panicked, and told him I had only seen dynamite in movies and knew nothing about how to use it. He shrugged this off and went on to show me what to do. Peel the wrapper off the putty-like dynamite (strictly against safety rules as it turned out), mold it into clever little wads, and press these into natural cracks in the rock. Learn that fuse burns at eighteen inches per minute, stick a fuse with a blasting cap in the dynamite wad, light it, scramble up out of the grizzly, turn on alarm lights and bells, holler "Fire!" and get around a right-angle corner to stay out of the way of rock fragments.

The crew stayed long enough to help me try a blast and left. I began to get the hang of it, carefully. Actually it seemed pretty exciting to a seventeen year old city kid. Best of all, it gradually let me keep up with the crew.

A hitch did develop. The proper procedure was for the grizzly man to sample each carload of ore before it was dumped, chip off samples, put them in a bag, and label them as to where they came from. There was an obvious disconnect between this procedure and the bonus system of pay. The leader had told me to forget this nonsense and to simply fill sample bags from the fine material that accumulated around the edges of the grizzly, and if time permitted, to store up a supply for the future. I was occupied in this chicanery when I sensed a presence. I looked up.

A figure leaned on the guard-rail of "my" grizzly and said, "Just what the hell are you doing down there?" I gave some smart-aleck answer and the figure responded, "My name is Norman McLeod. I am the mine captain here. Who taught you to sample in that manner?" I back-pedaled and said that I had invented this method just hours before, and wondered if anything was wrong. This caused him to burst out laughing, and he walked off. When the next train arrived, the leader told me the mine captain had spoken to him, but that everything was OK, except that maybe I should sample properly for a while.

At the end of the shift, exhaustion reached epic proportions. But after about a week, as my proficiency grew, I was accepted by my crew, The Dirty Dozen.

As the summer wore on, I watched the mining engineer and the geologist when their rounds brought them to where I was working. To me they were sophisticated authority figures doing the complex work of mapping out and planning the future development of the mine. If I needed any proof of what I had been taught at home, that education was the key to all things, it was staring me in the face. I got to know the geologist, and when he sensed my interest, he talked to me about his method for planning each round of development beyond the current workings. To me he was an accomplished man working at something that was obviously of great interest to him. To be able to emulate him was an idea that fascinated me.

I worked from June through mid-September. I started university with far more money than I would have thought possible. I returned to work at the mine the following summer after my freshman year.

As the plane took off returning me to civilization that first summer, I had an inexplicable emotional moment that I have never forgotten over the many years since. It was probably due to the fact that I was reflecting on my experience with my first "real job". I was likely replaying my mental tape about the dignity and satisfaction of work. About the elation and confidence that go with accomplishing something that at first appears impossibly difficult. About the absolutely vital role that teamwork and inter-dependence can play. About the truth of my family's views on the value of education. We are very lucky when we do not simply learn of these ideas early in life, but in addition become convinced of their validity.

At any rate, the money earned that summer gave me an entrée into higher education. I paid for the rest of my education myself by working during succeeding summer breaks.

Anton Chekhov got educated on his own as a medical doctor, and became a world-famous author. My accomplishments were much less than his, but they followed the same pattern. I got educated as a geologist on my own initiative and had a very gratifying career. There is something soul-satisfying in knowing that you can handle it yourself.

Educating an Earth Scientist

During my five years in college, I lived at home to save money. Home was diagonally across the city from the university and this required a combination of bus and streetcar rides. But that did not matter to me. I had achieved a goal inasmuch as I was a university student. I could use the rides to read or talk with other students. In winter I would get off at a transfer point to have borscht at one of the mid-town Ukrainian restaurants.

The university's education system followed the United Kingdom pattern of awarding either a "pass" degree in four years or an "honors" degree in five years. In the science faculty, the first two years were the same for both "pass" and "honors" programs. To be eligible for the "honors" program, it was necessary to achieve high academic standing in the first two years. To stay in the "honors" program once accepted, it was necessary to exceed a set grade-point average. The "honors" program in the last three years became progressively more specialized until, in the final year, only two subjects were taken. In that final year, there were very few lectures. Seminars led by students with a professor in attendance were the main teaching method. I was successful in entering and completing the "honors" program with a major in geological sciences, and with chemistry as my second subject.

I had chosen geology as my major for several reasons. I am not sure that I can recall my reasoning with total accuracy, but as best as I can put it together today, my thoughts were something like this. First, as I've already made clear, I loved science. Second, I had been impressed by the geologist at work in the mine where I earned enough money to start university. Third, I had an aversion to leading an ordinary life. I wanted to do something special. In the environment of that time and place, opportunities to break out of the mold of ordinariness were rare. However, it seemed to me that there could be adventure and fulfillment in a geological career, and that certainly proved over time to have been a very fortunate line of reasoning.

There is no doubt, using the jargon of the late twentieth and early twenty-first centuries, that I was a nerd. Good marks, high degree of class participation, modest social skills. For instance, I wouldn't have had a prayer of being elected president of any student body or activity. I played intramural soccer and skied, but little else other than academic pursuits. However, I felt I would find adventure somehow.

After my second year I made extra money by being a chemistry lab demonstrator and by working for the provincial Department of Mines on Saturdays, drawing up mine plans. During summer breaks I worked for the mine described earlier, on a field crew for the provincial Geological Survey, and in my final summer break as a geological assistant on an exploration crew with what was then the world's biggest mining company, International Nickel. Some of these were in themselves great experiences. Actually, work during summer breaks was almost as educational as the university itself, albeit in a different way.

For instance, working for the Province of Manitoba Geological Survey, we were flown to a remote location and when we started work, we found that the maps we had been supplied were worthless. Checking and re-checking made it evident that very little on the ground was as it was portrayed on the maps. A series of conversations with headquarters in Winnipeg solved the mystery, but the answer was almost incredible. The maps of this particular area had been made in the 1930's by a small cadre of geologists supervising large numbers of students from all disciplines in a Depression "make-work" project, in the area we had been assigned for detailed mapping. Students of art, medicine, journalism, and every discipline imaginable were told to cover field traverses making a "B" symbol on maps where they saw black rocks (usually basalt), an "R" symbol where they saw red rocks (usually granite), and so on, and the results would be sorted out later by geologists. We managed on the radio to find a geologist who had participated in the program. He told us that, first thing in the morning, the students would often disappear behind the nearest hill and find a comfortable spot to relax for the rest of the day while they filled their maps with symbols.

No one who planned our assignment knew of this crazy episode of the past and simply gave us the resulting maps in good faith that they were accurate. After all, they were printed in color on linen paper and signed by a senior officer of The Geological Survey of Canada. So, we started all over. I learned a lasting lesson. All may not be as it seems. Doubt, caution, skepticism, and wariness are all healthy reactions. If your senses tell you something is amiss, you should definitely snoop and pry and say to yourself, "Hold on! Why should I trust this?" no matter how official or proper the information is held to be. In fact, later in life this sort of skepticism saved me from bad situations more than once.

Working for International Nickel in northernmost Manitoba in my final summer break, I had the good fortune to be among the junior persons on the crew that located what would become the Thompson Mine, one of the world's largest copper-nickel deposits. This may have been the first (and certainly, at least, was one of the first) major metal discoveries made primarily by an electromagnetic survey. Such surveys induce an electric current into the earth and, by noting the patterns that such a current takes, detect buried ore-bodies that are electrical conductors. In this case the conductor was a huge deposit of pyrrhotite and pentlandite, the sulfides of copper and nickel. At that time the device used to induce the electric current and the receivers were back-packed into the area by human mules, of which I was one. Later, it became possible to conduct the same surveys from helicopters and fixed-wing aircraft.

I had some wonderful professors. One of them, Professor Edward Leith, was revered over a long career to the degree that The Ed Leith Cretaceous Menagerie opened in the fall of 2003 at the university. He was famed for bringing paleontology alive, and because he married a twenty-year-old student when he was well past fifty.

One of my memories of him relates to the fact that he called me MacVicar instead of McIvor. When I would say to him in class, "Professor Leith, you know my name is McIvor, not MacVicar," he would respond with a huge smile and say, "Of course I understand that, MacVicar. Now shall we get on with the great science of paleontology?"

Another professor, George Russell, was my self-appointed mentor. He straightened out numberless academic issues for me. When he was party chief of the Geological Survey crew that employed me one summer, he taught me how to exist in the unforgiving Canadian "bush" (North Woods to Americans).

Once when I accidentally smashed a vital compass, he had me walk out and back the thirteen miles to the nearest settlement, twenty-six miles in all, to pick up a replacement and send the broken one for repair. Ten or twelve hours alone on a narrow trail in the bush is a little eerie, and gives a profound sense of loneliness and being cut off from the rest of the world. However it made me feel in that regard, it did make me very conscious of being careful with vital equipment, which I suppose is what my boss wanted to impress upon me.

Still on the subject of vital equipment, the walk was also memorable because while I was squatted over a log to relieve myself, I was stung by about ten or twenty wasps. The little rascals must have had a nest in the log. I had (at least temporarily) the male vital equipment that I had always wanted. This painful situation did not make the walk at all easier.

The head of the Department of Geological Sciences, Dr. George Brownell, stays in my memory for at least two reasons. He was co-inventor, along with two physicists, Ralston and Pringle, of the scintillometer. This device measured radiation far more accurately than the Geiger counter of that time and at far smaller strengths.

Dr. Brownell taught us professional ethics, although that was not officially part of his Economic Geology course. He had decorated his classroom with framed prospectuses from fly-by-night mining companies whose aim was to sell stock in imaginary mining discoveries. They were written by stringing long, important-sounding geological words together with verbs, and promised quick riches. They were written by down-on-their-luck geologists, we learned. Dr. Brownell let it be known that he would haunt any of us who ever participated in such schemes.

To a naïve student, it was hard to imagine anyone getting this far down on his luck, but such is the innocence of youth. Some years later, I saw one of these scams actually take place, not by someone down on his luck, but rather by someone who was a con artist, a flimflam man.

Here is how it happened. During an oil boom in Southeast Saskatchewan, my wife and I and our first child were living in the small city of Regina. Our home was a tiny apartment above a drug store and we socialized periodically with neighbors in adjoining apartments. One pair of neighbors was not ordinary folk. The male, a recent Swedish immigrant, was a very dapper dresser and a glib talker who stood out from the crowd. His wife also stood out. She dressed in glamorous fashion, for instance, large "picture" hats in summer. It was actually a spectacle when they left together for work in the morning. They would both be stylishly dressed and he would open the passenger door and hand her into the car, unusual in that neighborhood.

One evening they came to visit us, and the man quizzed me about the oil business. I found it difficult to tell where his conversation was headed until I realized that he was looking for a way to get into the oil business. This was odd, since he styled himself as owner of an import-export company. I told him that getting involved in the oil business took a great deal of capital, and if his aim was to get into the Canadian natural resource business, that he might look into the mining business because it was far less capital-intensive. A good deal of uranium exploration was taking place in that part of Canada at that time.

Shortly afterward, I read extravagant claims by an entity called Lorondo Uranium Mines which sounded suspiciously like the "scams" Dr. Brownell had warned his students about. Then, one day my wife showed me a newspaper article that identified our neighbor as president of Lorondo Uranium Mines and noted that the company had declared bankruptcy. This was the time-honored procedure whereby a phony mining company would incorporate, get itself listed on a minor stock exchange that was not too rigorously regulated, sell stock in fictitious mining ventures described in complex geologic terms, and when it was judged that the market had absorbed all it would take, declare bankruptcy.

I had been an unwitting accomplice in the type of seedy venture about which Dr. Brownell had warned us. My neighbor studiously avoided me from that point onward. I never did find out the identity of the down-on-his-luck geologist who wrote the promotional garbage for Lorondo Uranium Mines.

Returning to my time at university, overall it was very stimulating and rewarding. It was a serious time rather than fun. Since I attended in the five years immediately after WWII, I turned out to be the only non-veteran in my graduating class. My classmates were in university because the Government of Canada offered them a free education, as happened in the United States with the "GI Bill." They were extremely serious people and I had to be serious to keep up with the pack.

I thought about graduate school, but there was a tremendous pull on me to get out into the big wide world and "do something." I had a strong desire to establish myself in some way.

In the early spring of 1950, campus recruiters visited. The Leduc oil field had been discovered near Edmonton, Alberta in 1947, starting Canada as a significant producer of oil and natural gas. (In 2003, Canada and

Mexico were the biggest and almost equal sources of United States' oil imports, not Saudi Arabia as is often mistakenly claimed). A representative of Exxon's Canadian affiliate (Imperial Oil Limited), the discoverers of the Leduc oil field, came looking for geologists. I was one of two students to whom he offered a job. I was such a careful individual that, with the job of a lifetime staring me in the face, I told him I would think about it. I came back next day to tell him that I would accept. He went on to be CEO of the company. And I did too. I replaced Jack Armstrong as CEO thirty-one years later when he retired.

I missed the graduation ceremony at my university. The city of Winnipeg was flooded by the Red River of the North that year and the graduation ceremony was postponed until fall. By that time I was about one thousand miles away, absorbed in my new job, and I didn't think a trip back was worth it. But I did receive a memento I treasured: the Science Faculty graduation ring, a plain oval, the only things on it being the name of the university and a question mark to remind us that a good scientist questions everything. Perhaps the designers of the ring had in mind the same thought as is expressed by the original motto of The Royal Society of London at its formation in 1662: *nullius in verba*, don't take anyone's word for it. The years ahead would supply me with much to question.

I unfortunately lost the ring many years ago. However, this year something told me I want to have it again. Perhaps it was writing this book. When I inquired from members of the Department of Geological Sciences, I found that the ring as a graduation symbol had long since been discontinued.

Then one day the department head, Dr. Nancy Chow, e-mailed me that the same manufacturer still did work for the university and could manufacture one for me if I confirmed the details of the design. I did so and was very happy to receive a new ring. I surmised that manufacturing only one ring would be expensive. It probably was, but Dr. Chow sent it to me with the note that the Department of Geological Sciences wanted me to have it as recognition of the help I have given students in the department over the years.

This event, perhaps minor to some, acted as welcome closure in regard to my reminiscences of my education.

Life on the Canadian Prairie

As a young Canadian earth scientist employed in oil and gas exploration in the 1950's, I got to know the small towns and the farms and ranches of the prairies very well.

The prairie of Western Canada is made up of portions of Manitoba, Saskatchewan and Alberta. It forms a huge triangle with a nine hundred mile east-west leg along the United States border abutting North Dakota and Montana, an eight hundred mile northwest-southeast leg along the Rocky Mountain front, and the even longer third leg (joining the first two) where the prairies border the rock outcrops and coniferous forests of the Precambrian Shield.

Canada as a whole is about five percent larger in area than the United States, but its population is only eleven percent as large. Further, about sixty-five percent of Canada's thirty-one million people are in Ontario and Quebec.

Only five million of Canada's people, or sixteen percent, live in the vastness of the prairie provinces. Going even further, most of these five million people live in the prairie cities. So, obviously, there are very, very few people living on the farms and ranches and in the small towns of that bald, flat, terrain.

I had the opportunity to get to know the area, its people and landscape quite intimately. I was born and raised in Winnipeg, lived in two Alberta small towns, lived four years in Regina, Saskatchewan, during an oil-boom in that area; and lived in Canada's oil capital, Calgary, Alberta, for eleven years in three separate periods. And of course I stayed in numberless fleabag hotels in any small town that happened to be near a seismic crew or drilling rig with which I happened to be concerned.

My first Imperial Oil Limited job, directly after college graduation, was based in a tiny Alberta town. The job merits some description, and so does the town, because there are so many like it.

One's first after-college job seems momentous to the individual involved. In my case, at age twenty-two, I had rarely been out of my home province of Manitoba. Cheap air fares and widespread student travel were still decades into the future. So traveling nine hundred miles to a place with which I was quite unfamiliar caused simultaneous excitement and apprehension.

When I arrived at Imperial's office in Edmonton, Alberta, I was briefed and then instructed to join a company seismograph crew based in the small town in question, three hundred miles north in the so-called Peace River Country, the northern prairie of Alberta. The crew was one of several in the general area attempting to locate bigger cousins to a minor oil discovery nearby.

As noted already, the town was typical of small towns on the Canadian prairie at that time. The population might have been about 1,500. It was a stop on The Northern Alberta Railroad, and had a couple of food stores, one restaurant, no hotel, two churches, and several farm-machinery agencies. The economy was strictly agrarian. I got a room in a house and ate breakfast and dinner at a truck-stop restaurant.

The heart of a land-based seismograph crew at the time was a truck containing instruments to record the shock waves generated by small explosive charges in shallow holes and bounced off sedimentary layers in the earth. We used two truck-mounted drills and two accompanying water trucks to bore the holes for dynamite, a so-called "shot truck" containing the dynamite and equipment to load it, a couple of trucks that laid out and reeled in quarter-mile cables to which the shock receivers (geophones) were attached, and the surveyor's half-ton vehicle.

The crew consisted of a party chief and assistant party chief who handled the recording, a surveyor and his helper, the shot-hole drillers, a shooter and his helper, the reel-truck driver and, lowest of all, the "jug hustlers" who handled the stoop-labor job of clipping the receivers (geophones or "jugs") to the cable after it was laid out and who removed them before the cable was reeled in after a "shot." The data obtained were shipped to an office where experienced earth scientists interpreted the information.

My five college years studying every known undergraduate course in earth science earned me the right to work as a "jug hustler" as my entree into the oil business. Unlike the elaborate and lengthy indoctrination courses offered to new hires during the previous forty years, my new employer thought starting as a jug hustler was the best way to get a thorough grounding in petroleum exploration.

Of the fifteen or so people on the crew, three were college graduates: the party chief and his assistant were electrical engineers, and me, the geologist-cum-jug-hustler. The other twelve were Alberta farm boys looking to do something other than cropping the family land.

There was a lot of interesting by-play between the locals and the seismograph crew. We were looked upon as aliens in the town.

Remember that this was in a period just after WWII. The first really significant oil deposits had just been discovered in Western Canada three years earlier. Small towns like this one had rarely seen outsiders other than a few itinerant salesmen.

There was virtually no social life. The nearest movie theater was fifty miles away. At that time, the only legal public drinking was in so-called "beer parlors" located in hotels which, amazingly enough, were owned by breweries. There were separate drinking rooms for men and women. When enough beer had been consumed, the atmosphere in the men's section often turned ugly. The only other social venue was the Saturday night dances. Asking a girl to dance quite often resulted in a brawl with one of the local swains.

Our one big attempt to ingratiate ourselves with the community was a flop. At around midnight one summer night, the town hall caught fire and when we tried to use our water trucks to help extinguish the blaze, we found ourselves very unwelcome. We never did figure out exactly why. We were merely puzzled onlookers, never to know.

I was amused that we would receive mail from the local headquarters in Edmonton painting the benefits of good corporate citizenship. However, these did not contain any instructions as to dealing with drunk farmers or being smart enough to recognize when not to meddle in local affairs.

How did I appreciate my first assignment? I was stimulated by it. I was out in "the real world" finding out if I could make my way in it. I liked the feeling.

After my next posting, a short assignment working in the exploration headquarters in Calgary, four other geologists and I opened a base of operations in another town in the Peace River Country, and this one was considerably larger. What was remarkable about it was that its normal population of about five thousand would at least double each winter when the muskeg terrain (read "swamp") north of the prairie froze, thus allowing transport of drilling rigs and seismic crews, which was impossible in summer. The town was the base for these operations for a very large territory.

How does a small prairie town accommodate a doubled population for half of each year? I lived with others behind a house in a garage which had been crudely remodeled into one room with several beds and a bathroom. Anything that could be rented was rented at rates that proved beyond question that scarcity results in high prices.

At mealtimes each of the town's restaurants was very crowded. My colleagues and I usually ate at a boarding house, which I still remember. The food was so uninspiring that one of my colleagues would bring paper napkins so he could wrap things he didn't care to eat and smuggle them out later in his pockets so as not to embarrass or anger the cook/hostess.

As time wore on and our operation expanded, the company towed in ten or so trailers as employee living quarters for the staff, which had now grown to about twenty-five. At about that point we began to become a part of town life, for instance, forming a softball team that played in the town league against teams from other oil companies, The Royal Canadian Mounted Police, and local businesses. As center fielder I was "good field/no hit."

Regina, the capital city of Saskatchewan, is a neat and tidy little prairie city and I have good memories of the time I spent there. The population was fewer than 100,000 at the time. I bought my first house here, borrowing even the down payment. It was a tract house on the absolute edge of the city and, until there was further building, we would see tractors and combines in the wheat fields, separated from our house only by the width of the street. Looking out our front window, we could see summer storms coming when they were still thirty miles or two hours away.

Just how flat the prairie is here can be appreciated from the fact that a railway line going southeast from Regina to the town of Stoughton, about seventy-five miles away, is arrow-straight and does not have a five degree bend or more than fifty feet or so of elevation change in the entire distance.

Living could be harsh in that environment. It is a semi-desert, with annual total precipitation (rain and snow combined) of only about fifteen inches. The average wind speed, 365 days a year, twenty-four hours a day, is in the order of twelve to fifteen miles per hour, so dust-storms and blizzards are commonplace in winds that often reach forty miles per hour.

Blizzards presented a real hazard. A significant number of farmers died each year by getting lost between the house and the barn. Those who were more careful strung a rope between the buildings. Many more died of carbon monoxide poisoning when they pulled off the road in their cars or trucks during a blizzard and left the motor running for warmth.

Part of my job was to make regular visits to four or five seismic crews scattered around the area. We were trained to never leave the city of Regina in winter without a sleeping bag, a survival kit with food and water, a snow-shovel and tire chains. We were trained to pull off the road in a blizzard and to simply wait it out by shutting off the engine and climbing into the sleeping bag in the back seat. Cell phones were not yet invented and no two-way radios were supplied, so a four-to-eight hour wait could prove to be pretty eerie. A battery radio helped, but not much.

The blizzards were curious in one way. Because the annual precipitation is so low, a blizzard is not usually due to new snowfall. Often it is due to the same six inches of snow blowing back and forth across the province from November until April. This dawned on me one night when I was flying back from one of my regular trips to the exploration and production headquarters in Calgary. When the Air Canada pilot announced we would be landing shortly, I could see the moon and stars very clearly. During the last two hundred vertical feet of descent, there was a sudden "whiteout." The engines came up to full throttle, and the pilot announced it would be necessary to go on to Winnipeg. This proved to be a common November-to-April happening.

Other than family and work, one of my interests during the time I lived on the Canadian prairie came each autumn when I could hunt ducks and geese and upland game birds. It has become very politically incorrect to admit that such dastardly behavior lurks in one's past. However, my family always ate what I shot, and the truth is that it was mainly an excuse to walk miles in the outdoors on autumn Saturdays. There is some ineffable awesomeness to being on the prairie, far from any habitation, particularly when one is alone. The sky stretches forever in all directions and the horizon is perhaps twenty-five miles away instead of a few hundred yards as it is in heavily forested New England.

When I feel sleepless, instead of counting sheep I sometimes replay my mental tape to recreate any of several such autumn Saturdays on the prairie.

One such recreation in my mind takes place at the base of the Rocky Mountain Foothills just southwest of Calgary. In my half-asleep, half-awake state I see myself get out of my car, leave my shotgun unloaded until I climb through the barb-wire fence, load the shotgun and begin walking through the grass westward toward the foothills. I change course a few degrees toward a bunch of small trees that may harbor a flock of sharp-tail grouse. As I get within about thirty yards, the flock bursts from the cover and I drop one. I put the bird in the inside pocket of my hunting jacket and turn toward where I think the flock landed. The eastern sun of early morning shines to the west on the beautiful slope of the foothills and the snow-capped Rocky Mountains behind them. It is pleasantly warm. I feel tremendously alive and comfortable and ——-zzzzzzzzzzzzzz—— I'm asleep.

Flying or even driving over the great North American plains can leave the impression that the landscape is dull and uninspiring. City folk in, say, Toronto, New York or Miami probably think of the area as being as uninteresting as any place on the planet. Having been born there, having had the opportunity to work and live in half a dozen prairie locations, and having traveled over most of it, I know how wrong that is.

The Duke and the Maiden

In the mid-1960s, in a tiny village above the Arctic Circle in Canada's Yukon Territory, was a very small radio station. The station broadcast local news to the inhabitants of the area, largely native people. The daily broadcast began at eight p.m., and the news was largely of local events, such as fur-trapping results. The young woman who ran the station would sign on with the announcement, "Good evening. Here are the news." She was one of a very few who had gone out to Edmonton, Alberta, to be educated. She knew that a plural subject demanded a plural verb, and thus "Here are the news." I thought this was actually quite a reasonable approach.

Then and perhaps even now, His Royal Highness Prince Philip, Duke of Edinburgh, traveled about the British Commonwealth periodically in something called, approximately, the Commonwealth Conferences. On one such tour through Canada, the Duke was making a swing through Arctic settlements, and the village in question was on the itinerary. The place was fairly abuzz at the announcement that it would be a stopover for an honest-to-God royal. Preparations were given top priority.

The young lady who ran the radio station pulled every string imaginable to be among those chosen as waitresses for the dinner that would be held. A guest list was assembled, including all local dignitaries. The dinner went smoothly. A welcoming speech was given and then the guests sat for the dinner.

Anyone acquainted at all with the inhabitants of the area would realize that while the Duke was treated with respect, he was hardly held in awe. Polite conversation and laughter filled the dining room.

The soup course was followed by the main course. The young lady in question had engineered events so that she would serve the Duke's table. At the conclusion of the main course, she was busy picking up dishes and naturally attended to the Duke first. She picked up his plate and cutlery, but picked out the fork and placed it back before him.

She flashed him a blinding smile and said sweetly, "Keep your fork, Duke. There's pie!"

Guests noted that momentarily, he seemed not to know how to respond. However, he recovered almost instantaneously with a big laugh. He took it well. Both he and the young woman looked pleased. This was her evening! The story has been told and retold.

Minus Seventy-Seven Degrees Fahrenheit

At one point early in my career, I invented a way to make velocity surveys in oil and natural gas exploration wells more efficient.

What is a velocity survey? The procedure at that time has long since been made obsolete by digital technology. But here is what it was at the time.

When an exploration well reached total depth, whether it was a discovery or a failure, it was useful to measure the seismic velocity of the rock column that had been penetrated. By this means the reflections observed on seismograph readings could be "tied to" or calibrated with the large changes in rock velocity which caused them.

This was accomplished by a seismic crew going to the well site and lowering a receiver (called a "sonde") into the well, stopping it at the points identified by the well-site geologist as major changes in rock type, and firing a dynamite shot at surface. The depth to the point being measured divided by elapsed time from surface to that point (distance divided by time) would be the average velocity from surface to that point. When many such readings were taken at various depths, the distance between any two points divided by the difference in elapsed time would equal the interval velocity between them.

Once when I was reviewing the results of a velocity survey in the local field office that was my base, it occurred to me that the interval velocities themselves might be as good a diagnostic tool of rock types as the drill samples (called "cuttings"), cores, and the electric and other logs run in the well. The problem was that the crew making the survey had to accept the well-site geologist's estimate of the depth of boundaries between rock types. This was often not too accurate at that point in the process because the boundaries are often gradational.

I reasoned that if someone skilled was on the velocity survey crew, that by plotting each elapsed time at the corresponding depth as soon as it was recorded and before the next shot, that person could define the changes in rock type and thus rock velocity more accurately. He would do that by calling for shots on either side of a boundary that had been roughly estimated, and by then gradually closing in on it, he could define it more completely. For instance, is it a sharp boundary or gradational? The trick lay in making the survey a controlled and iterative process whereby someone "closed in" on the boundaries instead of taking readings only at predetermined points.

My boss was enthused about the idea, and when I tried it in a test, it worked as well as had been expected. Rock boundaries were more completely defined, and rock velocity itself was shown to be as diagnostic of rock type as drill samples and electric logs.

As already noted, the procedure I described was made obsolete a few years later by a sonde which was both a source and receiver of seismic shock, and could thus be lowered into a well and would continuously record the velocity of the rocks it passed through.

However, at that time my reward for my inventiveness was to be required to go to all company velocity surveys in that area of Canada. Obviously, many of these fell in remote and inhospitable well sites. The location which supplied the title for this short tale was just north of the Alberta-Northwest Territories border (60 degrees north latitude) and the month was January.

A thermometer sat on a bracket on the outside of a window in the trailer that was my temporary work and living quarters. When I got up the first morning the thermometer read minus seventy-four degrees Fahrenheit. When I reasoned that the trailer must be leaking heat, I realized that the real atmospheric temperature must be even lower, and this was confirmed by a thermometer on the drilling rig floor (read drilling crew work space), which was about minus seventy-seven degrees Fahrenheit. I pitied the drillers having to work in those conditions. I at least could fly home when my little task had been completed and didn't have to last out the entire duration of the well as they did.

The lowest temperature ever recorded in North America was at Snag, Yukon Territory-minus 81.4 degrees Fahrenheit. In the spirit of the adage that "No good deed ever goes unpunished," by improving the efficiency of velocity surveys, I got to experience an atmospheric temperature almost as cold as the record. As a motivational reward for inventiveness, this reminded me of the Stalinist Russia of Alexander Solzhenitsyn's "The Gulag Archipelago".

Mentors

A well-run company, particularly one that relies on and rewards ingenuity, does well when it encourages those who are recognized as skilled veterans to be mentors to their juniors. My company certainly did that. As a result I benefited from this practice and enjoyed the learning that it offered. Some examples follow.

Working in western Saskatchewan in the vicinity of some earlier discoveries, I was paired off with a geologist fifteen years my senior. Not only was he a skilled petroleum geologist, he was a "character." He was individualistic and had some trouble blending into the ways of a huge corporation, but if given free rein, he could work minor miracles.

Waldo, a United States citizen, had served in WWII in the Pacific Theater in a Special Forces group in Burma, as I got the story, and this left him with a great fund of stories and a droopy left eyelid, apparently an aftermath of a tropical disease. On evenings when some drinking was taking place, I could quite accurately gauge the state of his inebriation by how far down over his left eye the eyelid had drooped.

At any rate, we were a team charged with locating oil fields in an area that up to that point had yielded only natural gas. In the year 2004, when natural gas is being sold in North America for around six dollars per thousand cubic feet, it is hard to think that at that time, in that area, it was deemed worthless because there was no pipeline or other infrastructure to get it to market.

When we entered the picture, we noted that exploration had followed conventional patterns. The most common earth-architecture situation for trapping oil and gas is an anticline, that is, a dome or local uplift over which a reservoir rock is bowed upward and thus can entrap petroleum when it can no longer rise as it floats on subsurface water in the reservoir (remembering that gas floats on oil or water, and that oil floats on water).

The drilling in that area had been conventionally located on top of subsurface domes or anticlines detected by the seismic method, but up to that time had yielded only natural gas in perhaps half a dozen locations. However, we could see none of the usual signs that this was a "gas only" area and there was every reason to believe that it should have generated oil.

Waldo was the big thinker of the two of us, being able to synthesize data on a broad scale to understand the regional picture. My task was to interpret seismic data to get a picture of the local earth-architecture.

After some time absorbing the data, and also making some more unwanted gas discoveries we, and particularly Waldo, knew that some radically different approach was needed if we were to discover oil.

Waldo asked me one morning, "Have you seen a log on any well here that had water in the Viking?" (The Viking Formation was the sandstone reservoir rock in question). I thought about it and replied, "No. I can't remember any such well. Have you?" Whereupon Waldo replied, "No. There isn't any such well. I've checked them all. So, think about this. We have been assuming that the Viking is a widespread 'sheet' sandstone and that the only way to find oil is to drill where it's pushed up over a dome. I'm beginning to think that the Viking sandstone is a big, long, narrow succession of old beaches that wedges out just up the regional slope from all these domes, and could thus be a 'pinch-out' trap. If so, there could be oil in the 'lows' between the 'highs.' Do you think that's a reasonable idea?"

I thought a while and replied, "I think that's a reasonable idea. But even if we can make a good case for it, I guarantee some will find it heretical. Drilling in the synclines between anticlines is not exactly conventional wisdom in our trade." Roughly translated, that meant, "Who is going to tell the boss?"

Waldo told me that if I could map the overall configuration with reasonable accuracy and thus locate a "low" between two gas-bearing domes or "highs," he would do the convincing.

On a wall in the office in my home in New Canaan, I have a framed Imperial Oil Limited map of the earth structure of that area as determined from seismic surveys in the 1950's. It is intended to illustrate a point. The map has an inscription on it. Here is what it says:

"Successful petroleum exploration requires both data and ideas. Ideas change as more data become available. Early exploration wells in this area were located conventionally on the crests of anticlines and resulted only in the discovery of natural gas which at that time (mid-1950's) was virtually worthless. It was not until the idea dawned that the Viking sandstone is a long, narrow, east-west complex of ancient sandbars that the concept was formed that the synclines separating the anticlines could be oil-bearing. The first well drilled in a syncline flowed light gravity crude oil. The original recoverable reserves of this field were 105 million barrels of oil and 285 billion cubic feet of natural gas. An idea that developed while exploration was in progress resulted in a very significant profit."

The inscription indicates that Waldo taught me a lot. He was a great mentor. He taught me that conventional "schoolbook solutions" to any issue could be inadequate, and that one should always imagine and compare alternate solutions before adopting a final one.

Shortly after the events described here, we lost Waldo in an aircraft crash. He had taken four young geologists on a field trip to examine some rock outcrops in northern Saskatchewan. The aircraft, a single-engine De Havilland Beaver, faltered on takeoff from a lake and crashed. Waldo, the pilot, and two others perished. The other two young geologists survived. I took part in the air reconnaissance which spotted the wreckage of the aircraft and the two survivors. I was very saddened to have lost an inspiring friend and colleague who taught me a lot about my profession.

To describe a second mentor, at the period in my career when I was making the transition from being a technical person to being an executive, a senior member of Imperial's exploration and production management was a gentleman who had an uncanny ability to always know what was happening in the purview of his responsibility. He would know on both a grand scale and in some detail, and in both operational and human issues.

Whenever I was troubled about something, either a personnel or a business/technical issue, at the approximate point where the issue became critical, this gentleman would somehow magically show up in my office. He was an informal person, and in a friendly and relaxed manner he would ask me something like, "Well, young man, how are things progressing in your world?"

After a while I became confident enough to tell him my concerns. He would then give me a thoughtful appraisal of the issue from his viewpoint, and my usual unspoken reaction would be, "Now why didn't I think of that?" When I realized that this was his method of teaching, I was flattered that he took the time and effort to do so with me.

He helped me to see through many issues that were important to me, and gave me instructions as to how to handle them in such a way that I sometimes almost thought the ideas were my own. I knew I had a master teacher and paid close attention.

At a later stage in my career, I was considerably nervous about being a witness in a hearing. In a totally unplanned fashion, I happened to cross paths with the gentleman in question and mentioned my unease with this new experience. I can clearly remember his advice on this issue almost verbatim. It went like this: "I'm not going to tell you what to say. But I will give you some pointers about how to behave. First, always tell the truth. Never try to shade what you know to be correct. It will always backfire on you. When you are under oath, perjury is a crime. The only other point I will make is that these hearings are by nature very competitive. It's always 'we' versus 'they.' That's why a hearing is being held. So here's a way to be competitive in this situation. The person questioning you for the opposition will be a lawyer. You know one hundred times more about the subject at issue than he will. He will ask you long, involved questions lasting several minutes. The object of his questions will be to pick your brain on the issue and then use your answers to make the points he has on his agenda. After any long involved question, which will really be a 'fishing expedition', simply answer 'Yes' or 'No' if you can, and then watch his confusion. He won't even remember what he asked you. He will be banking on the fact that most technical people are so eager to show off their expertise that they usually answer, 'No. It isn't really as you describe. Let me tell you how it really is,' and then he will twist your answer to his advantage. Why let your ego feed your antagonist?"

It seemed like an intriguing way to handle the situation. At the hearing, my interrogator acted as had been forecast. His annoyance when I answered his questions with a simple "yes" or "no" was obvious and then he would then look confused and say "All right. Then let's move on to something else". This made me feel a sense of empowerment. My mentor had taught a junior person how to deal with hostile questions from an experienced person. On that occasion and others, my mentor's advice worked just as he indicated it would. I did not get pushed into uncomfortable places and could choose my time to tell what I perceived to be the truth. I could not have admired my mentor more.

If I "did well" in my career, I have to acknowledge that I had some wonderful teachers. Realizing the value of mentoring, I tried to practice it with employees who worked under my supervision. The best memory of doing so came about years later when I left Imperial Oil Limited as CEO to join Exxon's headquarters staff as a director and senior vice president of the organization. Exxon's new CEO suggested that I should find the highest potential geologist and the highest potential petroleum engineer and bring them to the headquarters for two years or so to act as my staff. He reasoned that this would be a very positive learning experience, following which they would return to operations and be replaced by another pair. By the time I retired I had put four pairs through the process, and I believe they left with a pretty good idea of what information was critical to decisions at the headquarters level and how the headquarters functions. As this is being written, it is gratifying to note that two of the geologists who were involved are being named as president and executive vice president of ExxonMobil Exploration Company. It seems we picked the right people to mentor.

A Naif in the Third World: Angola

At age thirty, I was a satisfied earth scientist doing what I loved to do and being told that I was good at it.

Part of Exxon's corporate culture then (and probably still) is to place professional people on short assignments away from their home units if they have something to offer to a problem. This has a double benefit: it uses the best expertise to solve problems and it offers professional people wider experience than they would otherwise get.

I had never been off the North American continent and never owned a passport. My boss came to me with an offer from the parent company to be part of an evaluation team on an assignment in Angola, which was then still a colony of Portugal. A Belgian company had exclusive exploration rights to the entire country, had spent a lot of money with very limited success, and was looking for a partner. The other two team members were the parent company's most senior geologist and most senior petroleum engineer, both based in the Manhattan headquarters at 30 Rockefeller Plaza.

The plan was for me to do the dog-work, that is, to gather and organize the exploration data, do the geophysical interpretation (which the senior geologist was not equipped to do), and be generally useful to my very experienced seniors.

My first task was to get to the company headquarters in Rockefeller Plaza in New York City to meet my new colleagues and to get my marching orders. That was an adventure in itself, as I had never seen the great city.

At the time, getting to Angola from New York meant going to Paris, then to Nice, to Kano in Nigeria, to Brazzaville in the (then) French Congo, and finally to Luanda, the capital city of Angola.

In Paris, we met the president of the French affiliate to get his views on the Belgian company that would be our hosts in Angola. We stayed at the Hotel George Cinq, which looked to be the height of luxury to a young bumpkin from the Canadian west (and which still looks to be the height of luxury to me today.) The French president took us for dinner to a very good restaurant on the Champs Elysees. I sensed it had a nice, warm family atmosphere because there were so many elderly gentlemen present with their nieces.

As a geologist, I was awestruck flying over the Sahara Desert between Nice and Kano. After Kano, I was full of wonder when we had a stopover in Brazzaville, as my knowledge of Africa came only from movies. I got my first glimpse of the mighty Congo River, so wide at that point that I could not see the other side. Brazzaville is across the big river from Leopoldville, now Kinshasa, the major city of what was then known as the Belgian Congo. That year, there was a major rebellion against the colonial government which led to Belgium abandoning its colony. As we departed Brazzaville, the Air France pilot obligingly flew us over the Leopoldville Airport to show us where the runways were lined with bomb craters and burnt-out cars and planes.

Adventure was still to come before this voyage to Africa was complete. The Canadian Department of External Affairs had repeatedly assured me in response to many questions that no visa was needed for Angola. My new boss, in the next airplane seat, asked me on the flight into Luanda, "You have a visa, right?" I told him I did not, and he laughed and said, "We are going to have some fun!"

At the immigration desk in Luanda, speaking through an interpreter, the clerk told me that since I had no visa that my options were to get back on the airplane or be detained until someone in Angola would take responsibility for me. Thus it happened that I spent my life's only night in jail. I was released the next morning on the recognizance of the president of our host company, who thought the whole thing was funnier than I did. The Canadian External Affairs contact and I had a very spirited discussion when I returned much later.

My stay in Angola was stirring to a young man who was learning that he really liked this sort of thing. Once we got established in a hotel and learned the routine at the host company's office, we traveled in a Land Rover over most of the coastal area, getting a feeling for the terrain and the difficulty it would present to exploration and production operations. We spent time at drilling camps in the jungle where, in the middle of the night, I could hear drummers communicating with one another in the distance.

When we crossed what I remember to be the Catumbela River upstream from Benguela by loading the Land Rover onto a ferry powered by men with poles, I thought I had reached the outer limits of the earth.

One can easily imagine the effect this had on me, a naif who had never before left North America. Try to imagine the sensory effect of this journey. This was not a gradual change, but instead an abrupt transition from the comfortable environment of home base in Western Canada to New York City and Paris and then to sub-Saharan Africa, all in a few days, and then a tour around a country that was as foreign to me as it could be.

When I wanted to see a heavy oil deposit at the surface because of its possible similarity to deposits of that type in Canada, my senior colleagues acceded to my wish and decided to come with me.

The deposit was located in a coastal sugar plantation. Driving across the plantation in a Land Rover, we used narrow roads beside a narrow-gauge railroad that was built to take the sugar cane to the coast. Palmettos arched over the combined road/railroad rights-of-way, making them like dim tunnels. The driver, who I had already judged from his road habits to be certifiably insane, hurtled down them at eighty kilometers per hour. Drainage ditches crossing the roads and railroads had skimpy bridges over them.

About twenty-five yards from one ditch, the driver realized there was no bridge and the Land Rover made an arc through the air into the muck of the ditch. I flew out of the back seat into the neck and head of my boss, luckily, not breaking his neck. When we crawled out of the vehicle, the classic question arose, "What the hell do we do now?"

The last humans we had seen were Angolan workers about a mile back down the road. My elders thoughtfully nominated me to go back with the driver (who spoke Bantu) to recruit some help. I have a vivid memory of walking through the cane field and warily approaching the workers who, in turn, regarded us with suspicion.

The driver explained our plight and about ten of the workers came back with us. All of us stood silently around the accident, trying to think of a way to get the vehicle out. Ingenuity prevailed. We got the toolbox out of the vehicle and unbolted a length of narrow-gauge track. We then put a twenty-foot length of rail under the submerged front bumper and used it as a lever. About ten men hung on it and pried the bumper up enough to expose the winch. The winch line was hooked to several palmetto trunks until one held, and the Land Rover was out of the ditch, but on the wrong side! It took a lot of exploring to find a road back to the highway. We never did see the oil deposit, but I came away with some excellent photos of the rescue operation.

We worked well together with the Belgians. When we had absorbed all the available information and had asked all the questions we thought were important, we wrote a preliminary report in Luanda while we still had access to data. I still have the notes I compiled then in a credenza in my office. That done, we set off for New York to make our report.

Coming home from the assignment, we reversed the route by which we had come: Luanda-Brazzaville-Kano-Nice-Paris-New York and of course I still had the final legs New York-Toronto-Calgary. Commercial jets had just come into service on trans-Atlantic flights, but intra-Africa flights were still the propeller-driven aircraft of UAT, Union Aeromaritime de Transport, and the routes were not nearly as convenient as those that are now available.

On the seven separate flight legs returning from Angola to my familiar territory in Western Canada, I had plenty of time to stare out of airplane windows and to think back over what I had done. As I neared home I found it harder and harder to believe that I had just spent time in a very remote part of the African continent. As the title of this tale suggests, I was a naif, or, in cruder terms, a hick. It was utter good fortune at age thirty to begin to experience the huge world around me!

The French Connection

My first opportunity to get a meaningful conception of the French nation came about when I was asked in the 1960's to be part of a small team sent to visit Esso Recherche et Exploitation de Petrole, colloquially Esso REP. Our mission was to give an independent opinion of Esso REP's exploration effectiveness.

However, this tale will not be about exploration technology, but rather about how I came to know France. My only prior experience was a two-day visit with Exxon people in Paris on my way to Angola a few years earlier.

Esso REP had its headquarters in Begles, a village on the outskirts of Bordeaux. And that is why we took up residence in L'Hotel Splendide (which at that time was not very splendid at all) in Bordeaux. It was November and very damp-cold along the Bay of Biscay. The hotel had an archaic heating system and it was difficult to keep warm.

The concierge at the Splendide was a very old man, and he would tell me stories in the lobby at night. He knew little English and I spoke rudimentary French, but we managed to communicate in limited fashion. One story he told me that I have not been able to completely verify is that the hotel was a German general's headquarters during the Nazi occupation of France. If I understood him correctly, the General was Dietrich von Choltitz, the man made famous by the American book, *Is Paris Burning?*, by Collins and La Pierre.

At the end of WWII, von Choltitz was the Nazi commander in Paris and had his headquarters there at the Hotel Meurice. He had been ordered by Hitler to place explosives on all the great landmarks of Paris, like the Louvre and the Eiffel Tower, for instance. According to the book, each night Hitler would phone him and scream, "Is Paris burning?". Fortunately for all of us, von Choltitz was very fond of Paris and could not bring himself to do it. The book became a good American movie in the 1960's. At any rate, the concierge's tale fascinated me and I would sit in the lobby trying to imagine the hotel being the Nazi headquarters in that part of France.

Time away from work was interesting, and that is what this tale is about. For instance, chefs in Paris had no doubt been accommodating foreign tastes for centuries, but not the chef in L'Hotel Splendide. It was a mark of my lack of sophistication that I did not simply relax and enjoy French food, but at breakfast I grew hungry for bacon and eggs. When I ordered deux oeufs sur la platte avec jambon, I was given to understand that my request was impossible, and perhaps even an atrocity.

So, the next morning I asked if it would be all right if I cooked them myself. This brought the chef to my table with a couple of hangers-on. He would not deign to respond in kind to my fractured French, but sniffed, "Mais certainment! Can we humble novices watch this miracle?" So that is how it came to be that I was in the kitchen cooking my own breakfast with the chef and his minions making wise-ass remarks in French that they thought I didn't understand. I was careful not to abuse my privilege but periodically thereafter I would ask to cook my eggs and bacon and my wish was always granted.

Another of the visitors and I made friends with the chief geologist and his wife. The French had the same work schedule we did, Monday to Friday, and they would show us the local sights on weekends. On occasion this was memorable. One trip was to the nearby foothills of the Pyrenees to see 10,000-year-old murals in the limestone caves of that region. The caves were national monuments attended by concierges. At one that we visited, because it was very early in the morning, the concierge entrusted us to his teenage granddaughter. With a flashlight, she took us into the cave and asked us to sit on rocks in a given part of a grotto. When she shone her light on the wall, an excellent mural of a mastodon, head down and charging the viewer, appeared.

She then asked us to move about twenty feet and sit at another location so that we would now see the same mural from a vantage point ninety degrees different from the previous view. When she then shone her light on the same mural, we saw a beautiful woman. We perhaps tend to think of the humans of the last ice age as primitives. No doubt they were in some senses, but they obviously had great creativity, imagination, and artistic skill. Trompe l'oeil paintings have obviously been made in France for a long time.

This assignment left me wanting to know more about France. I got to do this in several ways. For one, my oldest son won a scholarship to L'Universite Paul Valery in Montpellier, just west of Marseille on the Mediterranean coast. He completed a Ph.D. degree there and then worked for The Organization of Economic Cooperation and Development in Paris; so he was in France for five years. This afforded me the opportunity to visit him many times, and by this means I got to see a good deal of Le Midi and Provence and the area around Montpellier in particular.

Several episodes from this time stirred my imagination and I retain strong memories of them. For one, on my first visit to my son in Montpellier, he took me on a tour of the university. The first point of major interest was to learn that it was founded as Europe's first medical school in 1137 and achieved university status in 1289. I thought my alma mater was ancient because it was founded in 1873!

In a large assembly room in the present day medical faculty, all around the wall are paintings of what today we would call the deans of the Medical School over the last 800 or so years. When my son asked me if I could recognize any names, I walked around them slowly, and of course stopped when I saw the name Francois Rabelais. That was my first inkling that the famous author was also a medical doctor. My son then showed me a statue in the courtyard, and it was of the man, in an obviously Rabelaisian pose, a wreath of grape leaves on his head and a wine goblet in his hand. The phrase "Renaissance man" and the word "polymath" began to take on a stronger meaning for me. Today we prize excellence in narrow specialization more than the ability to master more than one major field of endeavor as Rabelais and others of his time did.

Another notable event during my first time in Montpellier had to do with the fact that I had come there directly from a visit to Scotland. I had been looking at the area from which my family sprang in the Hebrides Islands and the northwest Scottish mainland. I visited the battlefield at Culloden, just outside Inverness, which battle (in 1745) ended Scotland's existence as an independent nation. I was interested because the odds are favorable that some of my antecedents took part in the battle, since the Scottish army was made up of civilian soldiers primarily from the northwestern highlands.

In the course of this visit, in recognition of my Canadian nationality, the guide pointed out that General Wolfe, who achieved fame at the battle of

The Plains of Abraham in Quebec, had been at Culloden as an eighteen year old officer in the Royal Marines. I marveled! James Wolfe may have directed fire at persons from whom I am descended.

At the battle of The Plains of Abraham in 1759 in Quebec, a significant action in The Seven Years War (French and Indian Wars to Americans), James Wolfe had been the victor over the French Forces under Louis-Joseph, Le Marquis de Montcalm, thus establishing Canada as a British colony. Wolfe was killed in the battle and Montcalm died of wounds on the next day.

When I described my northern Scotland findings to my son, his face fell and I could not guess what had perturbed him. Without explanation, he led me out of the hotel in which I was staying in the heart of the old city part of Montpellier. We walked a few blocks and he stopped at the gate to a very old mansion which, in the local style, had an interior courtyard rather than open property around it. We went into the courtyard, and on the house was an inscription on a cornerstone which read (in French) approximately: "In this house Louis-Joseph, Le Marquis de Montcalm, was born February 28, 1712. In 1756 he raised an army in this area and took it to the French colony of Quebec in Canada. At the Battle of the Plains of Abraham there, he died for the greater glory of France on September 14, 1759."

I was somewhat taken aback and almost began to believe in predestination. In the space of ten days, far from home, I had by chance (rather than on purpose) come across the tracks of both antagonists in a battle which determined that my country would become a British rather than a French colony.

I took many other vacations in France, and I got to make several more visits to Esso REP, as I did to all of Exxon's exploration and production areas after I became a Senior Vice President of the company.

Obviously I thought that France had a lot to offer in many ways. I have tried to master painting but have never gotten beyond being a crude dauber. However, this does not prevent me from enjoying visual art and my favorites are two French Impressionists: Claude Monet for landscapes and Pierre-Auguste Renoir for people. Thus the ability to see these and others in The Musee D'Orsay and L'Orangerie in Paris is something I have done several times and will do again.

France, and particularly Paris, exerted enough pull on me that in the summer of 1996 I lived in Paris for five weeks. I rented a flat on Boulevard Haussman and walked in all but one or two of that city's arrondissments, probably traveling over one hundred sidewalk miles, and saw Paris in the way I had always wanted. My favorite walk was around the circumference and down the central street of Ile St. Louis. Over the doors of many of the residences are plaques naming historical persons who have lived in them, and they conjure up images of what life must have been like over the many years that Paris has existed.

The United States and France have had a long close relationship dating back to our origin in The American Revolution. The animosity related to the Iraq War of 2003-2004 has soured this relationship. Although I share in this negative feeling toward France over this issue, I try to separate this from the warm memories I have of that country.

A Reluctant Executive

After twelve years with the company in a variety of technical positions, I was a happy man. I seemed to be recognized as a pretty good earth scientist. I had a wife and three children, and the bank and I owned a house.

My ambition was to be the best practical earth scientist the company had ever had. I held a very low opinion of managers, executives, and administrators. I thought of them as "suits" who occupied themselves at arcane, largely pointless tasks that made life complicated for truly productive persons such as myself. I had several offers to be a manager but had turned them down without giving them serious consideration. Why would I want to be a "suit" when I was so thoroughly enjoying what I was doing?

At this point, my life suddenly veered off in a new direction. The company had a 125-person exploration research group at the exploration and production headquarters in Calgary, Alberta. The manager, a Ph.D. geologist who had formed the group, died at a young age, and no successor had been groomed or even thought about. It was like a bolt out of the sky when the job was offered to me. I was incredulous. How could this be? I politely protested that I did not want the job, and gave the opinion that there were others much better trained and equipped than I.

However, a very frank talk followed, during which I was told that my next paycheck would be on the research manager's desk.

Whoa! Hold it! What's going on here? I didn't like this at all. However, sober reflection told me that with a wife and three children and a mortgage, I had to give this some serious consideration. Even if I didn't want the job, I did revere the company in general. It had been very good to me. But starting down the path of being an executive? My normally high spirits were dampened.

However, reluctantly but prudently, I said, "Okay, I'll try to be an executive." A promotion and a pay increase helped, but I was still very leery of my new situation. But I began to sit in the research manager's chair.

At first, the challenge was both daunting and confusing. The biggest supervisory effort I had ever undertaken was of six earth scientists traveling around the Canadian prairie pretty much on their own. Now I was responsible for 125 people, almost all of the professionals, among them more highly educated and more skilled in various specialties than I. It was obvious to me that I aroused suspicion. And why not? I had no credentials as a researcher, while the man I replaced was internationally recognized and the staff respected his memory.

All this was discouraging. Finding myself responsible for the attitudes, behavior, morale, and, in certain instances, the personal lives of 125 people left me insecure.

One morning at about five a.m. I got a phone call telling me that an expatriate employee had committed suicide and that I should quickly make sure that his family got all the support they needed. Some time later a group of senior employees told me that they felt one of their colleagues was mentally unstable, disruptive to the work place, and that I should devise a solution.

On a totally different level, I was expected to be the godfather at company social events, and the out-spoken geologist had to learn that "incredible!" was a preferable expression to "bullshit!"

And above all, there was the heart of my job: I was held accountable for and was judged on the basis of ensuring that the research program was directed at the company's best interests.

It was unsettling to be required to deal largely with abstractions rather than easy-to-grasp facts and actions. I had been used to gathering concrete pieces of information and synthesizing them into an action such as recommending that an exploration well be drilled or that more geophysical surveys were required before a technical issue could be resolved.

Now I had to grapple with issues like the performance and promotion potential of people, or with creating the best communication interface between research scientists and operations personnel, or guessing at how changes in operations factors would translate into research requirements.

More and more I had to deal with abstractions and people and less and less with measurable quantities and facts.

What a maturing experience this assignment turned out to be! I began to see that I had made an arrogant and superficial judgment as to the value of executives in the work place. Two things became clear. First, without skilled leadership, even the most capable groups can be rendered useless. Second, long-term survival in business, just as in life in general, relies every bit as much on cooperation and interdependence as on individual initiative.

I struggled through two years of being a neophyte executive with no horrible blunders and a few minor successes. I recognized that some wise person or persons had seen where I was headed and applied some corrective action. I remain forever grateful, whoever you were.

Hobnobbing with Colonels and Generals

In the early 1970's, the world paid a lot of attention to the findings of The Club of Rome, which forecast world shortages of most of the commodities that are critically important to our civilization, including crude oil. At the same time, political tensions in the Middle East made oil shortages seem quite possible.

It was for these reasons that the Canadian Armed Forces National Defense College (analogous to the United States War College) decided that its session for 1972-1973 should be significantly concerned with the availability of petroleum fuel. This seemed wise, as petroleum fueled Canada's tanks, ships, and aircraft just as it did everybody else's war vehicles. Someone further decided that a representative attending the course should be an expert in this field. No one in the military was deemed to be such an expert and so it came to pass that my company was asked to supply a candidate to be the energy expert at the upcoming National Defense College session.

I was never sure how I got to be that candidate, but somehow I did. Maybe it was my two years as the corporate planning manager. The appointment made me somewhat suspicious. I had been promoted rapidly and I wondered if I had screwed up and was being pushed away. But I was assured that it was being offered as a growth opportunity, and since the company continued to pay my salary it seemed obvious that is what it was. So I relaxed (sort of) and decided to make the most of it.

Home base for the college was Fort Frontenac in Kingston, Ontario. Since I was then based in Toronto, about sixty miles away, I could commute home on weekends.

There were thirty-six student attendees at the college. Twenty-four were from the military, most of them colonels or naval captains, one was a brigadier general and one was a naval commodore. Six were from the federal and provincial bureaucracies. Three were from private industry (the other two were from an aircraft company and from a railroad), and two from academia. One was the commandant of the Royal Canadian Mounted Police. Four of the military people were from allied forces: one from the United States, two from Great Britain, and one from Australia.

On the college staff, the commandant was a two-star admiral; the others Air Force and Army brigadier generals and colonels.

The format for the annual event was a forty-seven-week session (fifty-two weeks minus staff vacation), four major trips, and for the remainder of the time Monday through Friday, a.m. lectures and p.m. work on group projects.

During the session I attended, the major trips were in North America (Ottawa, Toronto, Montreal, Washington, New York, Fort Bragg); Latin America (Bogota, Brasilia, Rio, Buenos Aires, and Georgetown in Guyana); Africa and Asia (Calcutta, New Delhi, Agra, Nairobi, Yaounde, Doualla, Singapore, Jakarta, and Kuala Lumpur); and one to the Middle East, which I missed when I was called back to the company.

The lecture component of the course produced lively debates. This was the early 1970's when liberalism was at its peak in North America and traditional values were held to be politically incorrect. Thus I often found myself challenging the views of many of our guest speakers based on my rudimentary knowledge of national economics and on my business experience. It seemed to me that many speakers disdained economics except when it could be used to support a particular point of view. Most speakers made it clear that they disdained business.

The commandant sought to control the sessions by insisting that all questions and answers come through him in the fashion of the Speaker of the House in the British House of Commons. When any egregiously liberal speaker finished, the Admiral would say, "I expect on that note that Mr. McIvor will expose us to the full majesty of the free-enterprise system." And I would. I lost count of the number of times that I stood and said, "Admiral Davis, sir. I believe our learned speaker has perhaps neglected, etc." I was never sure whether I was taken seriously or whether I had simply become the entertainment.

The overseas trips were a highlight. The college had made some excellent connections around the world in its (then) twenty-six-year history. At each stop, officials from the local military, government or private institutions would host us and put on high-quality briefings pertaining to their particular nation or area. In this way, we usually met dignitaries of a high order throughout our travels.

Outside North America, most of the nations we visited were Third World countries. In the course of my career I had seen economically undeveloped nations before, but those exposures were always on my terms. That is, my prime concern then was oil and natural gas exploration and production, and when I was finished focusing on that subject, I could retreat to the warm cocoon of my safe and prosperous homeland. However, on the Defense College visits, the whole idea was to grapple (at least mentally) with what was often the abysmal living conditions for most of any nation's citizens, and thus with major social and economic issues.

I asked myself many times, "What would a young person in this country think about as he or she entered the work force?" And it was plain that mass communications, particularly television, gave vivid demonstrations to Third World citizens that life in economically developed nations was almost immeasurably better in a material sense and a political freedom sense than their lives.

All this led me thereafter to take a new interest in foreign aid, and by so doing, to realize that much or perhaps most of it serves to enrich those in control rather than those whose needs prompted my interest in the first place. This experience may have been part of the motive for my working for The International Executive Service Corps years later after I retired from Exxon. It seemed plain to me that the world would continue to experience war, insurrection and terrorism as long as gross disparities remained between the have and have-not nations in terms of material well-being and political freedom.

These journeys forced me to form a new perspective about the world. I took two major conclusions from them.

First, since we spent so much time in Third World countries I realized, as I never had before, the magnitude of the disparities among nations in material and other aspects of human life. In other words, despite previous exposure to these facts, it sank into my consciousness just how tremendously more fortunate we are in economically developed nations with democratic governments. I became much more conscious of what foreign aid could achieve, but at the same time disappointed by the degree to which it fails in its mission due to lapses by both donors and receivers. As already noted, this was likely the root of my post-retirement efforts at seeking a way to make a contribution to foreign aid that had some chance of working.

Second, we met many highly placed people, some of whom I had seen on television, and most of whom I had read about. In both developed and undeveloped nations, more often than not I was struck by their ordinariness. Celebrity seems to confer a special quality that was difficult for me to recognize and accept when I got the opportunity to meet and talk to celebrated people. Since then I have never offered the automatic deference that celebrity seems to command. I began to see that it does not really matter much what a celebrated person has done to achieve celebrity. It is celebrity in and of itself which matters.

I could now understand why, many years later when I sought to raise money for a cause, that I was told that my first order of business should be to get a celebrity to publicly back it. When I asked, "What sort of celebrity?" I was answered, "It doesn't matter, just get someone of celebrity status." When I gave a smart-aleck comment, "How about a serial killer?" my informant did not smile. But that is a whole other story.

The National Defense College experience was literally priceless. That is, there was nowhere else I could have paid to get the same breadth of exposure and experience compressed into such a short time and presented so skillfully. It gave me a much broader view of the world's people, resources, and economic and political systems, and it changed me as a person. I began to take an attitude toward many issues that was more tolerant and patient, but at the same time was more skeptical and questioning of what I learned from media sources. As I write about my change in attitude, I am reminded of Mark Twain's famous line, "Travel is fatal to prejudice."

There are three things we are born with that play a large part in our ongoing lives: our genes, our family of origin, and our citizenship. The Canadian National Defense College experience made me realize how lucky I was in my citizenship, and I gained a far greater knowledge of issues than is available to others not fortunate enough to have the same experience.

Class XXVI concluded in July of 1973. In April, before it concluded, the president of my company told me that I would be elected a director and senior vice-president and that I must return to work. Upon hearing the news, I went around to visit the commandant, the staff officers, and the attendees whom I had gotten to know best. I expressed my gratitude to all of them for the learning experiences we shared, and enjoyed the friendship of several among them for many years thereafter.

A Treasure House of Oil: Middle East Oilfields

If you pride yourself on your imagination, try to conjure up an image of an oil field that, on discovery, held ten times more recoverable oil than the biggest oil field ever discovered in the United States. The biggest U.S. oil field is the Prudhoe Bay field in Alaska, discovered in 1968. It then contained eleven billion barrels of recoverable oil. The Ghawar field in Saudi Arabia held 115 billion barrels at discovery in 1948. It is the largest oilfield ever discovered.

Everything about Ghawar is as perfect as it gets. To have it explained by people who are very familiar with it is awe-inspiring for a geologist or a petroleum engineer. I was fortunate to have such guides when I first saw it in the 1970's. If one's profession involves searching for oil and gas, then having the opportunity to see and understand the world's largest, most perfect example of one's quest is a major experience.

Now try a quiz question. The total number of oil fields ever discovered on Earth is about 30,000. That number is inexact, but it doesn't matter. Any bigger number would include a string of oil fields so small as to be insignificant. Now here's the question. How many of the 30,000 oil fields hold one-third of all the oil ever discovered? The answer is thirty-nine. Yes, thirty-nine. Only twelve of these are outside the Middle East.

How can this be? How can oil be so unevenly distributed on the planet that about thirty-three percent of all the oil so far discovered is in only 0.1 percent of the oil fields?

The answer lies in understanding that the factors necessary to form an oil field: an organic-rich source rock to generate the oil, a porous and permeable reservoir rock to house it, a rock-bed configuration to trap it and prevent it from leaking away, and a lack of destructive factors, such as overheating and erosion, are independent of one another in origin. Thus, to have them all occur together is rare. To have all of them occur together with optimum quality and size, as is necessary to trap giant fields such as occur in the Middle East, is extremely rare. It is the combination of circumstances that petroleum geologists dream of finding.

These factors obviously came together in the sedimentary rock basin surrounding the Persian Gulf. Looking at remaining reserves as of 2003 (United States Energy Information Administration figures), the oil fields of Iran, Iraq, Kuwait, Saudi Arabia, The United Arab Emirates, and Qatar contain about sixty percent of total world reserves. This concentration of such a vital commodity confers enormous geopolitical significance on this area. As far back as the time just prior to World War I, Winston Churchill surmised the significance of the then-new discoveries in the Middle East and insisted over strong objection from opponents in the government and The Admiralty that The Royal Navy convert its ships from coal to oil.

The table on the following page makes the geopolitical significance abundantly clear. It shows the world's five-biggest oil consumers and the five-biggest producers. Only the United States and the former USSR appear in both groups. The United States produces only forty-five percent of what it consumes, and must obviously import the remainder. The former USSR (virtually all Russia) consumes only forty percent of what it produces, so it is little wonder that oil exports are the backbone of its economy. The other three top consumers, as with the United States, rely heavily on imports, including one hundred percent reliance in the case of Japan. The five largest consumers are obviously the world's biggest economies, and four of them rely significantly on oil imports. Could the geopolitical significance of Middle East oil be clearer?

WHO CONSUMES IT & WHO PRODUCES IT?

THE WORLD'S FIVE LARGEST OIL CONSUMERS AND PRODUCERS

All figures in millions of barrels per day except percentage data from U.S. Energy Information Administration, 3rd Quarter, 2003

FIVE LARGEST OIL CONSUMERS		FIVE LARGEST OIL PRODUCERS	
United States	20.3	Persian Gulf*	18.6
Western Europe	15.2	Former USSR**	10.4
China	5.6	United States	8.8
Japan	4.9	North Sea***	6.0
Former USSR	3.7	Venezuela	2.6
Total, Five Largest	49.7	Total, Five Largest	46.4
Fraction of World	63.3%	Fraction of World	59.1%
World	**78.5**	**World**	**78.5**

* Saudi Arabia, Iran, Iraq, United Arab Emirates, Kuwait, Qatar

** Mainly Russia

*** Mainly Norway and UK

The chart also gives an idea of why the world has seen a significant run-up in crude oil prices during 2004. Most estimates of spare, readily available producing capacity in late 2004 are less than 5% of current production. Historically, whenever spare capacity has gotten significantly less than 10%, purchasers have expressed their concern about availability by offering higher prices. The current inching of demand toward producing capacity limits is generally attributed to a booming Chinese economy and a rebounding United States economy, while additions to producing capacity have not kept pace.

What is it about oil and gas that makes them so important to human society? About three hundred years ago, just yesterday in our progress from The Stone Age to The Information Age, the beginning of a major change occurred. Until that time, we had relied on animal and human muscle for motive power, and on burning wood, coal, and other materials for heat and light. In the brief span of time since then, people in the economically developed nations have come to rely virtually completely on coal, electricity, and oil and natural gas for the energy to fuel the countless activities that take place in their societies.

That they fuel economically developed societies is made evident by the almost perfect correlation between economic indices and energy consumption. The more highly developed the economy, the more energy it takes to fuel it. Going to each end of the spectrum to make the point, the United States currently has about $40,000 of Gross Domestic Product (GDP) per person and consumes about 60 barrels per year of oil and oil-equivalent energy per person. A group of nations at the other end of the spectrum (e.g., Bangladesh) has less than $400 of GDP per person and consumes about 1.5 barrels of oil and oil-equivalent energy per year per person.

Of all the energy sources, crude oil is the most vital to society because it is so versatile, and because for some of its many uses there are as yet no economic substitutes. The most critical of these uses is fueling motive power. Unless and until there is an economic substitute fuel to power cars, trucks, planes, and trains (for instance, using fuel-cell-powered engines), we cannot do without oil and still be able to sustain the developed economies, or offer the possibility of improvement in the undeveloped economies. And, as world population continues to grow, the need for oil grows with it.

The use of oil's handmaiden, natural gas, has grown rapidly in the last fifty years, largely as a low-pollution source of heat energy.

Thus, in oil, we have what is arguably the world's most critical commodity at the beginning of the Twenty First Century. It is vital to the continuation of the societies we have built, and is as yet irreplaceable for some uses upon which these societies depend. Oil's extremely uneven distribution among the world's nations and societies, together with its indispensable nature, combine to make its importance to us hard to exaggerate.

Even when I confront an issue as critical as the concentration of oil in the Middle East, together with that area's political fragility, the petroleum geologist in me sometimes makes my mind stray to Lee DeGolyer, who is regarded by many as the dean of American petroleum geologists.

DeGolyer led a remarkable life. Born in a sod hut in Oklahoma, he enrolled in the University of Oklahoma. While still an undergraduate, he took time off for a job in Mexico, where he located a well which discovered the first oilfield in The Golden Lane Trend along the Gulf of Mexico.

The discovery well flowed at 110,000 barrels per day, probably the highest per well flow rate ever achieved. One is forced to wonder what grades he was given by his professors when he returned to his studies at the University of Oklahoma.

During World War II, Harold L. Ickes served as the U.S. Secretary of the Interior and also as the Petroleum Coordinator for Defense. Ickes called on DeGolyer to make an appraisal of the oil potential of Saudi Arabia and other Persian Gulf nations.

In his Pulitzer Prize-winning history of the oil industry, *The Prize, The Epic Quest for Oil, Money, And Power* (10), Daniel Yergin describes how "DeGolyer mastered the art of eating sheep's eyes when they were ceremoniously offered to him ...The physical hardships were worth the trouble many times over... He was overcome by excitement, for he recognized that he was investigating something for which there was no precedent in the history of the oil industry. Even he, who had discovered a well that flowed at 110,000 barrels per day, had never seen anything on so vast a scale."

I have tried to picture what went through DeGolyer's mind as he gradually absorbed the magnitude of what he was seeing. How I envy his experience.

Xinjiang Autonomous Region China, 1987

Of all the experiences I had in foreign cultures, the outstanding one was a trip to a very remarkable part of the earth in a remote part of China. It combined intrigue, wondrous sights, opportunity to learn, and some understanding of Chinese politics and culture from close up.

Xinjiang Autonomous Region lies in the extreme northwest of China. Its other official name is The Peoples' Autonomous Uygur Republic. This name reflects the fact that the largest ethnic group in the region is Uygurs, a Turkic-speaking Islamic people, with most of the remainder being Han Chinese. (The Uygurs speak a Turkic language. As I understand it, this is not because this area was ever conquered by Turkey, but because the Turks originated here.) This huge area (about 640,000 square miles, 2 1/2 times bigger than Texas) is very sparsely populated because it is almost totally a desert and has climatic extremes, as much as plus 125F degrees in summer, as low as minus 50F degrees in winter.

Its boundaries are interesting: on the south, the Himalayas of Tibet and India; on the west, Pakistan, Afghanistan, Tajikistan, and Kyrgyzstan; on the north Kazakhstan and Mongolia with its own Gobi Desert; to the east, China proper. Marco Polo's Silk Route to China was through Afghanistan and Xinjiang.

Early in 1987, one of the Deputy Prime Ministers of The People's Republic of China visited my company's headquarters in Manhattan. He was also minister for all forms of energy and minerals and, like me, a geologist. He was a person of heroic stature in China, credited with the discovery and development of the Daquing and Shengli oil fields that made China self-sufficient in oil for a period. He was extremely interested in western oil exploration technology.

Xinjiang Province was then held to be the most attractive area of China to discover new oil fields. The popular press had run articles to this effect, and in the past we had teams visit the area, but not much information was made available to them. So we really had little solid information on which to form an opinion. In a joking way, the minister chided the company's CEO and me about the fact that I had never personally checked it out. It seemed obvious that he wanted us to make an offer and saw a visit by a senior group as a means to bring this to a conclusion. To cap things off, he offered to make all technical data accumulated by the Chinese national oil company available to us. When the CEO said to me, in the minister's presence, "Why don't you?" the venture went into play.

The Minister made arrangements for the president of our exploration affiliate and his senior expert on China, our representative in Beijing, and me to be his guests to evaluate the oil and gas prospects in Xinjiang Region.

On our arrival in Beijing, the minister showed us the greatest courtesy. He held a dinner for us in The Great Hall of the People, the most luxurious building I have ever seen. In attendance were the highest officials who had anything to do with Chinese energy issues. In his speech, the minister announced that we would be invited to present a plan for exploration in Xinjiang at the conclusion of our tour. His announcement was a total surprise to us. First, we had not expected to be asked to make an offer so quickly. Second, we thought he would want dialogue with us prior to an offer on our part. But when I checked with him after the meal, he confirmed, without explanation, that this was the way he wanted to handle it. Since at that time there were opposing viewpoints in the Chinese hierarchy as to foreign investment in petroleum exploration, he may have wanted to get an offer out on the table among his peers. I kept the CEO informed and told him we would check any offer with him prior to presenting it to our hosts.

And we were off. From Beijing, we flew to Urumqui, the capital of Xinkiang. After Urumqui, we visited every oilfield and exploration site in this vast area by small aircraft, helicopter, and Land Rover. We slept and ate in government guest houses, since there were no hotels in the area at the time.

In the far reaches of the desert, some guest houses had mud floors, no heat, and no running water. At one such stop, each of us received two huge thermos bottles of hot water every morning. These were meant to be used to make tea, but I would use most of it to clean up and shave.

All settlements were around the desert's edge, and we traversed the desert's circumference in two Land Rovers. This is a large distance and I calculated later that we spent perhaps fifty hours in the vehicles. While this was uncomfortable, we certainly saw wondrous sights, including a city buried beneath shifting sands about 5,000 years ago and uncovered when the prevailing wind changed direction early in the Twentieth Century; the mighty Tarim River thundering out of the Himalayas and then quietly disappearing in the desert; an ingenious system of dams that catch the spring runoff all around the desert's mountain rim and then trickle it slowly down over the growing season to produce a wonderful array of fruits and vegetables; the ancient city of Kashgar where Marco Polo entered China from Afghanistan; caves in the Flaming Mountains containing Christian frescoes from about 1,000 years ago; and towns with scores of pool tables in the streets because it never rains.

There were no roads in the desert's interior, so we had helicopter transportation in Russian Tupolevs that had no safety belts, but for some reason did have lace doilies on the seatbacks. When we reached a seismograph team in the desert center we found them working in terrain that had dunes hundreds of feet high. Frequent work stoppages occurred when the wind picked up velocity and caused sandstorms, reducing visibility to a few feet.

At most significant stops along the way there would be a dinner in our honor, and the senior persons acting as our hosts ranged from the Governor of Xinjiang Province to an oil field supervisor.

Chinese dinners of this type are filled with oratory (in our case all done with translators, of course) and protocol. The protocol is followed rigidly. The guests must line up outside the entryway in order of status to be greeted by the hosts, who are similarly arranged.

The socializing room outside the dining room is always furnished in exactly the same fashion. At the far end from the entry door are two chairs with a small table between them, facing the door, and the sides of the room have chairs arranged along them. Walking beside each other toward the seats of honor, the host invariably beckons the senior guest to the left-hand chair, and when both turn around and sit down, the guest is on the host's right. The host then gestures to tea or soda water on the table. After a sip or two, the host and guest exchange speeches and pleasantries.

Following this polite exchange, the hosts usher the guests into the dining room. After a few bites and chews, the host gives another speech, and the two groups then take turns raising their glasses and offering toasts to one another.

This protocol is apparently followed by China all over the world, since I found out much later that it held exactly true in the Chinese Consulate in New York City.

On nights in the desert when there were no formal dinners, the available entertainment was not quite as interesting. One night, I won a considerable sum of money from my colleagues by picking up, without any breaks, the greatest number of shelled peanuts with chopsticks without dropping one. Any fool can pick up peanuts in the shell, but shelled peanuts are difficult.

At one gathering, we got an especially interesting view of a narrow slice of Chinese culture. An English-speaking Chinese overheard us telling a joke, the standard American-type joke with a buildup that leads to a punch line. He asked what has caused all the laughter at the end, so we tried to explain the idea of what we call a joke.

He then suggested that since Chinese love jokes, the group should tell each other (through an interpreter) samples of this type of humor. It was a disaster. We would get our English-speaking host to translate an American joke and the Chinese would look at one another in puzzlement, and give a weak laugh out of politeness. They would then tell their English-speaking colleague a joke in Chinese and he would translate it for us. It turned out that the two cultures have a completely different idea of what constitutes a joke. A Chinese joke is more like a horror story about ghosts in the attic, but it does not build toward a punch line as ours do. So, like the Chinese, we would smile politely and compliment the teller on his humor.

Sometimes cultural differences came up in more serious ways. At an oil field at the southern rim of the desert, we had long technical discussions with the chief engineer who was in charge of the operation.

At one point, the engineer/manager asked me a series of long, involved questions. Bearing in mind that all this took place through a translator, I was puzzled about where his questions were leading. The point that I finally got was that he wanted me to describe how we supervised petroleum technical employees in "The West." Now I understood what he was curious about. As oilfield manager for the China Oil Ministry, he was responsible not only for employees' professional activities, but also for all other aspects of their lives: permission to get married, living quarters, health care, the dining hall, and even the communal laundry.

When I explained the freedoms of our citizens and the fact that we paid them enough that we expected them to look after their own personal lives, and that we supervised only their work performance, he went on at length as to how much he envied me as a "Western" manager.

A few weeks later I heard echoes of the same issue in Beijing when a young Chinese asked me, "What is it like to follow a religion?"

At yet another location, there had been serious natural gas blowouts and explosions, first in the original well and later in relief wells drilled to control the situation. Several people had died in the accidents. As an English-speaking petroleum engineer described this to us on the windswept plain around the blowout craters, he laughed several times. My surprise was apparently evident. In an aside, I asked our Beijing representative what was laughable about people dying in the accidents, and she told me that Chinese often laugh when embarrassed. Since my surprise had apparently been noticeable, I apologized to the engineer for my inappropriate reaction to his comments.

With a week left to go before the minister's deadline, we returned to Beijing with maps, cross sections, and hundreds of pages of notes. We showered, ate hamburgers and French fries, and settled in to review our assessments of the oil and gas potential in Xinjiang, and the offer we would make.

On the appointed date and time, we arrived at The Great Hall of The People for the dinner and presentation of our offer to our hosts. A motor cavalcade drew up at the door where we waited, flags fluttering on the front fenders of the limousines. It was dark at eight o'clock on a November evening, and we became confused when a hubbub ensued around the second-from-the-lead car.

As it turned out, the excitement was caused by the fact that the minister was having a heart attack in the car. I was very concerned. I genuinely liked and admired him and I knew he had suffered previous heart attacks. Finally, the deputy minister approached and told me that without the minister, there would be no point in presenting our offer. So we sat at the dinner talking about American baseball, Chinese history, and many other matters, all carefully unrelated to the petroleum potential of Xinjiang province.

After our return to the United States, we got word that the minister recovered. I arranged for our Beijing representative to hand-deliver a copy of the offer to him. He sent word that he was favorably impressed by it. However, he was replaced shortly after and with that we lost any encouragement to press on. When I retired six years later the matter was still not settled. Then, after that time, foreign investment in Xinjiang oil and gas prospects became possible and Exxon participated. Having no first-hand experience, I cannot comment on the results.

However, China has ceased being self-sufficient in oil because of the demand created by a booming economy on the one hand and not enough additions to China's indigenous oil reserves on the other.

All in all, the journey was a remarkable life experience for my colleagues and me. We interacted in a different culture and we learned a lot about how other people conduct their lives.

One event took place that made me think that we are all bonded together, despite our differences of culture, language, and political organization. At an earlier referenced oil field we visited, the chief geologist told us one night at dinner that there was a sight nearby that he wanted us to see the next day. He refused to tell us what it was, preferring to surprise us.

Thus, early on a cold November morning we drove several miles to the foothills of the Himalayas and then climbed six or eight hundred feet up the slope. We visitors had no idea where we were going or what we were about to see. Finally, as we came around a rock-corner, the chief geologist stopped and gestured to a vertical wall of what was probably Jurassic-age sandstone. There, going up the vertical wall were the preserved tracks of a three-toed pterodactyl, the leather-winged giant reptile of the age of dinosaurs. We shared a joke that the bird must have been very talented to walk up a vertical wall, knowing full well that the vertical sandstone slab, caught up in the uplift of the Himalayas, had originally been a horizontal beach when the tracks were made.

Our host was obviously proud to show us this treasure. Whatever the cultural and other differences there were between us, this small episode illustrated that we shared one bond, and that was our interest in the wonders that our profession revealed to us.

The Last Days of the U.S.S.R.

In the last years of its existence as a political entity, I visited the USSR several times. Mikhail Gorbachev was President, and glasnost and perestroika were in vogue. Although Exxon had been encouraged to explore the possibility of investments in USSR oil and gas considerably earlier, those efforts came to nothing. However, we now sensed that the time might be appropriate to open discussions once more.

On the first of these visits we managed to obtain an invitation to meet with Lev Ryabev, the most senior person in the USSR's energy hierarchy. He was one of several deputy prime ministers and was responsible for all forms of energy: oil, natural gas, coal, and nuclear power. He was a nuclear engineer, and Gorbachev had earlier chosen him to supervise the cleanup of the Chernobyl disaster in the Ukraine. We spent several days with him and with his staff in his Kremlin office, but this led to no concrete agreement to press forward with opportunities in the USSR.

A later, second visit was with the senior people in the oil ministry, GAZPROM (the natural gas corporation), and the geological ministry.

In these two visits we got to discuss several areas for possible investment: the Ob River Basin in Siberia, at that time the site of the largest oil fields and the source of the most production; and the Pacific offshore from Sakhalin Island where large oil and gas discoveries had been made, but where the hostile environment had prevented development and production.

It was clear that if any agreement was to be reached regarding our active participation, there would be a long period of negotiation, because there was obvious ambivalence on the part of the Soviet officials about the desirability of having this happen. The desire for and the utility of

"Western" technology and capital was obvious, but this was offset, it seemed, by a reluctance to have foreigners become established in the endeavor after years of being a state-run industry.

The only concrete outcome at that time was an opportunity to work on the data from an oil field that had presented technological problems. This gave us a chance to illustrate what we could accomplish, but in a very limited way.

The USSR ceased to exist on December 9, 1991. Our discussions continued with Russia and some former Soviet Republics. I retired early in 1993, and after that time Exxon, and later ExxonMobil, became a major player in this arena. I was gratified to have taken part in Exxon's entry into an area that has such a large presence in the world's energy future.

After I retired from Exxon and became an officer of the International Executive Service Corps, I visited that organization's operations in transferring American business expertise to activities in St. Petersburg, Warsaw, Prague and Budapest.

Throughout these journeys into Eastern Europe, I was conscious that I was given an opportunity to see a part of a major world event, the transition from state-owned economies to at least some degree of private ownership, and some degree of democratic government.

When one considers that there were seventy-something years between the beginning of the USSR and its dissolution, it is small wonder that the changeover to a very different system has not happened rapidly. An optimist with a long view might be impressed with the degree of movement toward creation of better economic conditions and more political freedom that has already occurred, given what came before.

On a purely personal basis, my greatest regret about Russia and the former USSR came about while I was working for the International Executive Service Corps. A professor at the University of Alaska (which has a campus in the city of Yakutska in the Autonomous Republic of Yakutskaya) asked me to accompany him on a journey there. This was to fulfill a request to assess the possibility of developing some oil and gas deposits there for local consumption to avoid the high transportation cost of bringing petroleum products from European Russia. Yakutskaya lies between China on the south and the Arctic Ocean on the north, somewhat inland from the Pacific (actually the Sea of Okhotsk). A very small population of Yakutsks lives in this vast land.

I found the idea exciting. Unfortunately, numerous crashes of Aeroflot flights (the only access) had led the pilots to go on strike. Our source of funds, the United States Agency for International Development, was barred by the State Department from paying for our expenses during the pilots' strike and I never got the opportunity to follow up after the problem cleared up. It has always been difficult for me to resist opportunities like that one, but it apparently was not meant to be.

The USSR and Russia have loomed large in our consciousness in The West, particularly since WWII. Although my visits there were not very productive of anything of great significance, the opportunity to see parts of it and to meet with citizens there allowed me a somewhat better understanding of the world in general. I look back on the experience as a positive one.

Why Do We Perform Better in Adversity?

All during my adult life, it has seemed to me that in virtually any endeavor, the participants perform in a more superior fashion under adverse circumstances than they do "when the good times roll."

It seems that, particularly in the world of commerce, long periods of prosperity and periods free of trouble induce sloppiness and inefficiency. The demand for labor of all kinds, from CEOs to minimum-wage jobs, becomes great enough to absorb all the labor that is available, regardless of its quality. It becomes less necessary to be proficient to stay employed.

For instance, many of the business strategies formed in the glow of prosperity in the late 1990s and the earliest years of the twenty-first century (before the bursting of the stock market bubble and the economic slowdown), drove some huge corporations into deep trouble. These follies are retrospectively evident even to those without business experience. In tougher times, I believe those involved would have thought more carefully, or someone else would have thought more carefully.

Going back to the 1980's, in the oil industry a lot of very expensive bets were made on ever-increasing prices. When reality reintroduced itself, there was a priceless bumper sticker in oil states like Texas which read, "God, please send me another oil boom. This time I promise not to screw it up."

As an example of the type of reckless behavior that took place in the boom of the late 1990's and the first year of the twenty-first century, numerous "dot.com" companies had hugely successful initial public offerings. Investment dollars poured in despite the fact that even a business neophyte could see that prospects for revenue, let alone profits, were based on little more than dreams and wishes. It is not at all surprising that many collapsed shortly thereafter. A cynic might say that they were never meant to succeed anyway, but many people got rich on the stock price run-up of the first day or two of the offering.

In a "boom" atmosphere, the average level of rational judgment used tends to decrease. It all looks too easy. Adversity, rather than comfort and ease, promotes ingenuity and cleverness. This brings to mind a wonderful book titled, *To Engineer is Human: The Role of Failure in Successful Design*, (8), by Dr. Henry Petroski, Professor of Engineering at Duke University. His thesis is that many great engineering advances result from disaster. As examples he describes the collapse of the Tacoma Narrows Bridge, the collapse of a catwalk with hundreds of people on it at the Kansas City Hyatt Regency hotel, air crashes such as the explosion of the De Havilland Comet (the first commercial jet airliner), and many others as the inspiration for significant engineering advances that have benefited human beings.

Stephen Jay Gould, who died in 2002, was one of my heroes. I believe he was one of the most inventive and provocative thinkers of his time. He pointed out that ninety-six percent of all species that have ever existed on the planet are now extinct, and that without the extinctions, evolution to ever higher forms of life (including homo sapiens) would never have been possible. There would not have been space or incentive. (He refers to this as "life's cruel little joke").

Thus, there seems to be widespread evidence that adversity promotes higher levels of achievement among living things. This observation may be no more than affirmation that the survival instinct is perhaps the strongest of the instructions that DNA imprints upon our genes.

I had a personal experience that made the reality of this idea completely evident to me. In 1981, I returned to Exxon's Canadian affiliate as CEO after a four-year absence at Exxon's headquarters. The biggest challenge facing the Canadian oil industry then was that the federal and provincial governments, who control natural resources, were convinced that oil prices would spiral forever upward, and they would make sure that they, and not oil companies, would be the beneficiaries.

The federal government's National Energy Program levied a Petroleum Revenue Tax on oil and gas production. The corporate income tax remained in place. So, revenues were taxed, and if this left anything that exceeded cost and resulted in a profit, it would be taxed again. The provinces (which owned the natural resources within their boundaries) had been caught up in the same fever and had increased their royalties on oil and gas production.

There was also a significant economic recession at this time so that petroleum marketing and refining also became far less profitable, as did chemicals.

Exxon's Canadian affiliate's earnings sank from about $450 million (US) in 1980 to a little over $200 million (US) in 1982 as a result of these factors. This was the largest decrease in the company's earnings since The Great Depression. As the new CEO, I wondered why my nickname was not "Lucky".

And there was an equally threatening issue looming. Canada's greatest reserve of petroleum lies in very heavy oil that occurs at or near the surface in Northeastern Alberta. The company had already begun commercializing these deposits by means of a multibillion-dollar mining and upgrading operation with other companies.

For several years, the company had been actively planning a second venture to commercialize these resources on a wholly owned basis. This venture would produce oil from shallow wells by applying high-pressure, high-temperature steam to reduce the oil's viscosity, and then upgrade the produced sticky bitumen into light oil in an expensive refinery. The total cost, as reckoned at that time, for both the producing and the refining facilities together, was about $12 billion (Canadian) and rising as the planning progressed. Although it had originally been planned as a wholly owned venture, as the costs began to rise significantly, partners were sought.

It was evident to me that even if we took an interest of less than fifty percent, we would need major changes in the fiscal regimes of both the federal and provincial governments, a very optimistic forecast for future oil prices, and the undertaking of a huge debt load in order for this project to proceed and be profitable. In effect, I could see that we would be betting the future of the entire company on a single project, and that if any of the assumptions proved to be significantly in error, the company could be bankrupted. Thus, my first major decision as CEO was to cancel it. This was understandably disappointing to employees who had placed great effort into designing it, and to governments who saw it as a source of jobs in a depressed economy. However, we also put out the word that if a way could be found to rejuvenate the project, it would receive close attention. How it was reborn is described later, and forms the crux of this essay.

With this threat behind us, I turned my attention to broader matters. For instance, I thought a lot about the organizational style of the company and about the people who made it work. I traveled extensively around the organization, and I talked to as many people as I could. For several years, the company had what I considered an excellent indoctrination program. Employees with about two years service were brought together in groups of about fifty and had the opportunity to have dialogue with middle- and upper-level managers on up to the CEO in order to get a first-hand idea of how the company functioned. I attended several of these to find out how people who had not had time to form biases felt about the company.

An opinion began to form as a result of this and other experiences. We had committees for almost everything, as though an individual were incapable of any decision. And we had what we came to call "paralysis by analysis", that is, we analyzed every possible action well beyond the point of diminishing returns. It was evident that our culture was far more comfortable with the process of decision rather than decision itself. The bureaucracy necessary to accomplish all the committee work and analysis was not only very expensive, it seemed to be stultifying progress, substituting procedure for action. This translated also into the fact that there was almost unlimited negative authority and very limited authority to make positive decisions except at the very highest levels.

I had for many years been in the habit of writing myself memoranda. It helped me to think clearly. It is hard for me to tell myself in print the foolish things I tell myself in thought. Weaknesses jump off the paper and beg to be corrected. Here is a sample of what I wrote to myself at that time: "I believe we should actively promote entrepreneurship, creativity, innovation and the undertaking of reasonable risks. We must try to identify and eliminate any impediment in our system that could get in the way of people making their maximum contributions." It appeared to me that the bureaucratic, over-analytic, process-oriented style rather than a results-oriented company culture had to change. It was expensive and crippling. Analyses and procedures are absolutely necessary to decision-making, but we had carried them to punishing levels.

I spoke to groups in the organization to convince them that significant change was necessary. I did not portray it as a matter of choice. I said that in the circumstances it was an absolute necessity. I made videos on the subject that were distributed to all employees.

Sometimes there was even humor, which helped. At one of the first conversations, which was with the twenty-five or so of the most senior headquarters people below our senior vice president level, a man stood up with a question and a comment for me. He said, "I am really impressed with what you are suggesting. But what I can't figure out is how you intend to get rid of bureaucracy. What do you propose? Will we have a committee?"

There was a deadly and lengthy silence as it sank in that the man was serious, and then the room exploded with laughter. The poor man looked stricken when he realized what he had said. I told him that he should be proud because he had performed a miracle of communication. He convinced us all how deeply ingrained were our bureaucratic instincts. I went on to say that there would be no formula to be applied, but that we should all think about what we were trying to do and then act on it, and that he should pay attention to me and to the senior vice presidents, who would be in deep trouble if we did not become models of what we were trying to achieve. The whole thing became popular, no hype, no propaganda, just practice being effective at your job and don't be afraid to try new approaches.

If there was opposition, it was in "the big middle." Some middle-level managers were threatened by the thought that their empires would dissolve, which they often did. At the highest and lowest levels, what was being suggested was adopted with enthusiasm.

We got a lot of help from the news media, who earlier had been negative about oil companies, particularly the one I worked for. When we began to get positive results, the country was eager for some economic success stories. The most positive media coverage appeared on the first business page of *The New York Times* issue of June 26, 1984. The NYT did not often cover Canadian business items. However, the reporter, Douglas Martin, painted a picture of the beginnings of a corporate turnaround brought about not by magic, not by the latest business fad, or not by legerdemain, but by simply being alert, innovative, and good at what we did. It did wonders for employee morale, including mine. I have it framed on a wall in my office at home.

Here is how the heavy oil "mega-project" was reborn. The oil-producing part of the operation was totally modular and could be accomplished in units of any size, including a single well, just to be ridiculous. The hang-up was the refining-upgrading plant, which had to be huge in order to have the economies of scale, and which accounted for the great bulk of the cost.

A clever group of petroleum engineers and executives came up with a solution that was beautiful in its simplicity: Don't upgrade the heavy oil. Mix it with readily available, light, low-viscosity condensate (gasoline-like liquids that are by-products of natural gas production) to thin it enough to go through a pipeline, and then send it to refineries in the northern tier of U.S. states that were already refining similar material.

We started it up with two small modules at a cost that was, as I recall, about $200 million or 1 1/2% of the original cost estimate. When these two modules made enough profit to support two more, we went ahead with them, and so on. As modules were added, the oil production rate increased until it exceeded what we had expected from the originally proposed giant project. The whole new venture grew in this fashion until it became the Canadian affiliate's single-biggest profit center.

At the time we began the first two modules, the Petroleum Revenue Tax was scrapped. What had been quite evident to us all along was finally broadly realized, that is, the tax worked against new investment that would compensate for the natural decline of existing oil and gas fields. To offset the effects of the tax, we had been concentrating on cost cutting, since this increased profit but not revenue. But now we could once again carry out projects that generated additional revenue.

Why did it take a major threat to make us conceive of this far more appropriate and economic means to resolve this issue? Rather than a change in physical factors, the big difference was the recognition of the danger of proceeding with the original plan. Simply put, we were frightened into scrapping it and using creativity to design a better one.

In trying to puzzle out cause and effect in such matters, I have already noted my layman's observation that the human brain functions more effectively under adversity. All along, I have felt that what is being described is not simply after-the-event learning from mistakes. What I am describing is real-time handling of events as they occur.

Over the past several years, I have become interested in neurology and brain function. This interest came about largely as a result of noting some of the amazing findings resulting from the ability to observe human brains reacting to stimuli through such advances as Positron Emission Tomography (PET Scans).

As part of this interest I came across the book, *Why God Won't Go Away: Brain Science and the Biology of Belief*, (7), by Andrew Newberg (a neurologist) and Eugene D'Aquilli (a psychologist). Their main thesis, that human beings have developed biologic adaptations to allow them to experience transcendence, religion, myths, and heightened awareness as survival mechanisms is interesting enough. However, the following quote from the book got my complete and undivided attention. The context is a discussion of how the neurological functioning of the human brain allows us to handle fear and anxiety:

"Thankfully the same big brain that generated these fears also provided a way to resolve them through intervention. Humans developed tools, weapons, and simple technologies. They banded into groups, allowing them to hunt cooperatively, share resources, and more efficiently defend themselves against hostile outsiders. They also invented ideas to protect themselves: laws, cultures, religions, and science, which allowed them to adapt more and more to their world. All the lofty reaches to which human achievement has carried us, from the first flint spearhead to the latest innovation in heart transplant surgery, can be traced to the mind's need to reduce the intolerable anxiety that is the brain's way of warning us that we are not safe."

Astounding! A biologic explanation for why we perform better under adversity! Reading that passage gave me one of those rewarding "Eureka!" moments when something one has observed to be true from empirical factors turns out to be supported by scientific observation.

Dealing with Risk

In a 1789 letter, Benjamin Franklin wrote: "...in this world nothing is certain but death and taxes." Mr. Franklin could well have written that nothing is certain but death, taxes and risk. We must all deal with risks great and small throughout our lives. There is no way to live risk-free.

Spending a career in the world of commerce and science makes this more than normally evident. In particular, exploration for oil and gas may be the only commercial endeavor (or at least one of a very few commercial endeavors) where the participants expect to fail most of the time. This quickly brings risk into focus.

But let us consider risk in a broader context. Whatever the nature of risk may be, one learns that it is insufficient to simply recognize and accept it. It is necessary to seek to reduce it to the greatest degree possible. By this it is not meant that risk should be reduced by avoiding it. Usually it must be accepted; but once this happens, some effort to reduce it to acceptable proportions must be expended. Oil and gas exploration technology is essentially a tool to reduce risk, to maximize the chance of finding economic oil and gas deposits. Petroleum engineering technology is essentially about formulating depletion plans for oil and gas fields, and designing and installing systems and hardware to accomplish them in the most effective manner possible. This usually means reducing the risk of all the many negative things that can happen to the execution of a depletion plan and its associated equipment.

In any business, it is necessary to establish how risk will be handled. Companies that are strongly risk-averse can be so cautious that they avoid making investments in the future to the degree that they have no future.

At the other end of the spectrum, companies that take extreme risks, for instance betting their entire future on a single project, assumption or action, can go bankrupt if these fail. Thus, it is necessary to establish where in the risk-averse/ risk- tolerant spectrum the company wants to be.

Having become conditioned to thinking about risk in business, it is easy to begin thinking about risk in all of life's aspects. For instance, sorting out the risks and rewards of the U.S. stock markets is an interesting case in point. Because so many Americans are now represented in equity markets by means of mutual funds and 401K accounts, the all-too-many cases of corporate fraud and malfeasance of the past several years have hurt not just a few wealthy investors, but a large number of everyday working people. According to *The Economist*, more than half of all American families are represented in the equity markets. All investors, the wealthy few and those who look to the market for a way to provide for retirement, must assess the risk that equity markets will continue to provide a reasonable basis for investment. Will new regulations really prevent future actions of the type that ruined the share value of many companies? That issue is unfolding as this is being written.

Having a significant number of citizens as owners in the economy is an important part of the American ethos, and is in sharp contrast to nations where the economy is owned by a much smaller fraction of the population. In the entire history of mankind, no one has ever washed a rented car.

For this large public ownership in the economy part of our ethos to continue and expand, there is a need for the public to be reasonably assured that the intrinsic risks of the equity markets are not compounded by the type of fraud and malfeasance to have taken place.

The great philosopher-psychologists-Freud, Jung, Rank, and Eriksson-saw psychological development in terms of risk. Each saw personality developing in stages, with individuals either passing successfully through each stage and going on to further development, or not doing so and thus carrying forward negative baggage to the next stage and perhaps for life. The relationship to risk is that as individuals come to each stage; either they confidently undertake the risk of the onward journey or, lacking confidence, become static or regress in their development.

Otto Rank saw those whose psychological development is most complete and who are confident enough to accept risk as "artists:" creative, individualized, and with integrated thoughts, feelings and actions. Those whose development is most stunted he called "neurotics:" hostile, arrogant, isolationistic, critical, guilty. Those in between he termed "average person": conforming, dependable, superficial, self-satisfied.

Genetics, nurturing and education equip some to deal confidently with life's risk, lead others to avoid it, and lead still others to take senseless risks out of desperation that is often politically or financially based. For instance, people at the lower end of the socioeconomic scale are attracted to lotteries. State-run lotteries are in my view the worst kind of political deception. They are a way to get persons who pay very little income tax to contribute more to government revenue. The New York State Lottery's television ad catch-phrase, "Hey! You never know!" is particularly offensive to me. In fact, if you were familiar with statistics and risks, you would say, "Hey! I do know." What you would know is that a New York State Lottery ticket buyer is seven times more likely to be struck by lightning than to win big at this game.

I watched a Columbia University professor of statistical mathematics be interviewed on *The Discovery Channel* on this subject. For dramatic effect, he was filmed standing on the windswept roof of a New York skyscraper which had free space down to the ground on all four sides. He held up a twenty-five cent piece in one hand and said, approximately, "You can blindfold me and whirl me around several times and then let me throw the quarter over whatever edge of the building I happen to be facing. If there were a paper cup on the pavement on only one side of the building, the odds that the quarter would land inside the paper cup are about the same as the odds of you winning top prize in the New York State Lottery."

In Las Vegas, I tried an experiment with slot machines. Ten dollars bought a roll of forty quarters. I got many rolls and kept feeding them, plus whatever winnings accumulated, into one machine until none was left.

I tried the experiment on perhaps five different machines. The object was to find out how many quarters could be fed into one slot machine until they were all gone, and the answer varied from about fifty to about three hundred. But what was absolutely certain (that is, zero risk) was that within a short time they would all be gone. If that were not true for the slots and all other offerings, how would the glitzy palaces stay in business?

The most fascinating, useful and brilliant example of risk management I know has to do with how a man dealt with the risk of his own death. As noted elsewhere, Stephen Jay Gould is among my pantheon of heroes. I was originally drawn to his work because he made what is perhaps the most significant contribution to evolutionary biology and paleontology since Darwin. He did this by realizing that biological evolution did not take place at a slow, more or less constant rate as had been thought, but at a generally slow rate punctuated by rapid bursts during which new species were created and existing species rapidly changed. The bursts of creation and change follow mass extinctions, because the extinctions create the space and the impetus for rapid evolution, and, as new and changed species take up more space, evolution slows again to what we previously thought was the normal pace.

As I absorbed this information I became aware that Gould had written much more broadly about a wide range of subjects. The risk management in question in this tale is described in his 1996 book, *Full House* (4). In 1982, at age forty, he was diagnosed to have a rare and (he was told) "invariably fatal" form of cancer known as abdominal mesothelioma. After his original surgery his doctor refused to recommend any reading that would allow better understanding of his condition.

So Gould, being highly curious, took it upon himself to search the literature to find why his doctor had refused to recommend reading for him, and to form his own prognosis. When he did so, he was initially horrified. He was a professor at Harvard at the time, and the medical school library had a brutal message for him: mesothelioma is incurable and median mortality is eight months following diagnosis.

Fortunately, Gould's curiosity about evolution and other matters had made him expert in the distribution of natural populations so he was skeptical about what "median mortality" actually meant in this case. For those not familiar with the term, in any population, half the members will be above the median and half below (in age, height, length of time from diagnosis to death, or whatever value is being measured.) The mean or average is obtained be adding all the values and dividing by the number of cases, and the mode is the most common value.

At this point, Gould's curiosity had led him to a destination that may have been the most important one of his life. This quote from *Full House* (4) explains:

"I then had the key insight that proved so life-affirming at such a crucial moment. I started to think about the variation and reasoned that the distribution of deaths must be strongly 'right-skewed' in statistical parlance...that is, asymmetrically extended around a chosen central tendency, with a much wider spread to the right than to the left. After all, there just isn't much room between the absolute minimum value of zero (dropping dead at the moment of diagnosis) and the median value of eight months. Half the variation must be scrunched up into this left half of the curve between the minimum and the median. But the right half may, in principle, extend out forever, or at least into extreme old age.

"I needed, above all, to know the form and expanse of variation and my most probable position within the spread. I realized that all factors favored a location in the right tail...I was young, rarin' to fight the bastard, located in a city offering the best possible medical treatment, blessed with a supportive family, and lucky that my disease had been discovered relatively early in its course."

Gould reports that he then checked the data on mesothelioma and confirmed his supposition: the variation was remarkably right-skewed with a few people living a very long time after diagnosis. And he saw no reason why he should not be among those inhabiting the right tail of the distribution. This was a precious gift at a crucial moment: the prospect of substantial time to think and plan and fight.

Stephen Jay Gould died at age sixty on May 20, 2002, twenty years after his initial diagnosis. What a magnificent example of a human being using curiosity, creativity and intelligence to understand and manage risk.

The very fact of being alive carries a lot of risk with it. It is an absolutely inescapable part of living. Since we can't be risk-free and alive at the same time, the only recourse we have is to use our capacity for rational thought to understand it and to use our creative abilities to manage it. Being frightened by risk is acceptable. That's probably what leads us to do something about it. Experience can lead to doing something about it very well.

Landscapes

Landscapes can pique our interest and can fill us with awe. As to stirring our interest, anyone trained as a geologist tends to see landscapes as objects needing explanation, objects of intellectual curiosity, and as such they present the gift of never needing to be bored.

For instance, flying over a lake formed by a dam, a series of V-shaped triangular inlets along its shore will be apparent, giving a "lace-edge-on-the-handkerchief" pattern, rather than the smooth contours of a natural lake edge. The reason is that the water level behind the dam has been raised (sometimes hundreds of feet) above the level of the river that was once behind the dam, and has backed up into the tributary stream valleys and has created a series of "V" shapes along the lake's edge. Once this diagnostic pattern is noticed out the window of an aircraft headed downstream, a dam will soon be in view.

Being a hunter of waterfowl and upland game birds gave me the opportunity to examine some landscapes in much more detail than I might have done otherwise. Most bird hunting is in relatively flat terrain that one would normally not find too interesting. But in walking what must be a few thousand miles for this purpose, I saw many landforms that stirred an urge to figure them out.

For instance, the southeastern part of the Canadian province of Alberta is a semi-desert, with mean average precipitation of less than twenty inches per year. But the area is covered by grain farms and cattle ranches thanks to intensive irrigation. Over several years, I walked over many, many miles of this terrain and thus had reason to try to decipher it.

The irrigation system was put in place in the early years of the Twentieth Century and was thus constructed with horse-drawn scoop shovels before bulldozers and similar equipment had been invented.

As I understand it, the irrigation water was taken out of the Bow River valley by a series of weirs. The valley is several hundred feet deep. At each weir, a channel was dug along the river's edge allowing water to spill in from the weir. By having a downward slope slightly less than the grade of the river, but still dropping, a channel will bring river water up out of the valley and onto the dry prairie several miles downstream from where it began. Once the water is up at prairie level, the trick became digging irrigation canals that keep water flowing downhill to the land needing irrigation. All this was done before aerial photographs, satellite images and radar had accurately mapped the elevation of the prairie.

As I would walk along the edges of the canals hoping to scare up ducks around the next bend, I was filled with admiration for the engineers who, with rudimentary surveying methods, figured out the course for canals in order to make ten thousand or more square miles a productive grain-farming and cattle-raising area.

Landscapes are also the source of an ineffably emotional feeling of awe. They are natural works of art on the thin and wrinkled skin of the planet. Even though we correctly see them as resulting from tectonic forces; of wind, water and frost erosion; and of the profusion or complete lack of vegetation; they speak to us of the beauty and drama that nature creates without any help from humans. They represent something greater than we are. They reduce us to mere specks on the skin of a big sphere. They teach us respect.

Going now to the absolute extreme southeast corner of Alberta, up against the Montana and Saskatchewan borders, the landscape is made up of gently rolling hills and valleys. There are clumps of poplars here and there in the valleys, but eighty-five percent or more of the area is treeless grassland with three-foot bushes and weeds along the fence lines of the cattle ranches.

I was last there in the autumn of 1998, when I went on a trip to recreate upland bird hunts I'd had forty-five years earlier when I was in my mid-twenties. I had told the outfitter that I wanted to hunt in exactly the same places I had hunted long ago, which he managed to arrange.

The experience stays vivid in my memory. It rekindled the feelings I had nearly half a century earlier. It was an unseasonably warm October, freezing overnight but reaching into the seventies during the day. By seven a.m., we would finish breakfast in the tiny town where we stayed and would be out in the hills behind the dogs by eight o'clock.

The days were windless and still, and I was reminded how intensely deep blue the sky can be in that area, how sharp and clear the air can be, and the fact that the horizon is twenty-five miles away from the viewer. All this is viewed in almost complete silence, broken only by occasional sounds from cattle or even more rarely from a truck on one of the gravel roads. The vista of the gentle hills rolling away to the south into Montana and to the east into Saskatchewan moved me strongly.

In his book, *The Golden Thread* (6), Bruce Meyer described how contemplating nature can transform us into a state of awe and an aura of contemplation and reflection that is far beyond facile explanation.

That certainly describes how I felt on that occasion. There were five of us hunting: a Newfoundland sea captain, an Alaskan forest ranger, an ex-deputy minister of the Canadian federal government, the outfitter, and me. We walked behind the dogs from eight a.m. until the last light had faded in the evening. At age seventy, I was the oldest person by twenty years, but I never felt fatigued or caused the others to slow their pace. The scenery made me feel as though I were breathing pure oxygen.

The most spectacular and dramatic landscape I have had the privilege to see lies in Yemen. In 1985 I went there to get final agreement from the president of Yemen (Al Abdallah Salih, who is still president) for an agreement by which Exxon and another American company would jointly develop an oil discovery there and explore for further discoveries.

The discovery lies east of the capital city of San'a under the Marib Desert. It is near the boundary with the Rub' Al Khali, "The Empty Quarter" of Saudi Arabia, which itself has spectacular 1,500 foot high sand dunes.

To get the oil to market, a pipeline was proposed from the oil field to the Red Sea. This meant traversing a mountain range, and while taking a helicopter flight along the proposed pipeline route, the terrain at issue came into view.

There must have been significant rainfall in the past to have formed streams to cut the spectacular valleys and to produce the mesas that exist. However, today and obviously for some time past, there has been very little rainfall and very little erosion, so the cliffs and canyons are as stark and un-rounded as they could be, and are unadorned by anything but scrub vegetation. There are many vertical rock faces of 1,000 or more feet along canyon walls and the edges of mesas. Part of one vertical face is the rock equivalent of the oil and gas reservoirs under the Marib Desert. It was fascinating to fly slow passes in the helicopter just a few feet away from the outcrops and think that within a few score miles these same rocks held great fortunes in their pores.

It is the stark angularity, the lack of vegetation, and the lack of any sign of human culture that made these cliffs so spectacular as they baked under the absolutely cloudless sky.

Very similar landscapes were filmed (I believe in Jordan) as the scenes for many parts of the movie, Lawrence of Arabia. On a road trip from San'a to the oil field in the Marib Desert, I passed through the canyons and mesas described, and I was made aware that a powerful sheik lived in a very unusual home carved out of the rock forming the top of one of the mesas. An offer was made to see the house, which I accepted. The vertical wall of the mesa in question was 1,000 feet and perhaps 1,500 feet from the rim to the flatland below. A rudimentary road with many switchbacks gave access to the top of the mesa on its gentler back-slope.

The rooms in the house were on two levels carved out of the very top of the rim-rock, and their glassless windows faced out onto the flat desert far below. Access to the rooms was by a staircase going down from the top of the mesa, in effect, a stairway entry through the roof.

The rooms were spotlessly clean. Running water of a sort ran from a cistern on the roof, or perhaps (given the lack of rainfall) from a well, and was distributed through the house by means of open channels in the walls that sloped at a slight grade. The women of the house ran and hid as we entered, and the sheik did not appear to greet us.

The attraction of the house over presumably hundreds of years was that the resident sheik could see a dust cloud from an approaching group when the group was still many miles away, giving him time to prepare.

I have a beautiful three foot by three foot framed satellite image of this entire area on a wall of the office in my home and it forms a very effective conversation piece.

Many more landscapes in my mental file have moved me or piqued my interest. Some that quickly come to mind were in Normandy and Burgundy, in the Loire Valley, the English Cotswolds, looking southward at the Himalayas from China, in Tuscany, on the Italian Amalfi coast at Ravello, the Canadian Arctic Islands, and scenes I can remember from skiing above the treeline in the Canadian Rockies at Banff and Lake Louise.

But to me, the most awe-inspiring images of nature are of the cosmos, in particular recent images taken by the Hubble Telescope. My sense of awe comes from contemplation of the almost unimaginable vastness of what is being viewed, the infinitesimal smallness of planet Earth in the cosmos, and the obvious order that exists in the system.

In *Just Six Numbers* (9), Sir Martin Rees, Astronomer Royal of The United Kingdom, makes the point that only six numbers govern the existence of the universe, and that if any one or more of the numbers were even 15 percent different, the universe could not exist.

The numbers are N, the electrical force that binds electrons together divided by the gravitational force between them; E, the force that binds electrons and protons to the atomic nuclei; O, which measures the amount of matter in the universe; L, the force of anti-gravity discovered in 1998; Q, the ratio of the gravitational force binding any two masses together to the combined weight of the two masses; and D, the number of dimensions in the universe, which is three.

If I accept that it is true that the universe is this finely tuned, then I am tempted to believe that that there is some overarching order to all things, a force that is likely The Higher Power that we have all sought to understand since consciousness occurred in homo sapiens.

Second Act: Dabbling in Academia, Foreign Aid and Consulting

A long career with one company has become a rare experience. When a 43-year career all in one company comes to an end, when one has loved it and done well at it, it is a reasonably traumatic event. An enormous part of one's life has been invested in it. Even if considerable thought and preparation have taken place, the finality of the event when it actually arrives is accompanied by considerable emotion. The emotion is not concentrated in any single event like a retirement party, but unfolds gradually over considerable time.

To pick just one aspect of this, I view Exxon as a superbly managed organization. Particularly in its treatment of employees, its culture is well understood by those working there, and that culture is transparent and fair. So, the end of a career there that lasted from college graduation until age sixty-five is like emerging from a protective cocoon. The world at large does not play by the same rules. In fact, it takes emergence from the cocoon to fully understand just how good it was.

What does one do when a career that has been stimulating and rewarding in so many ways comes to an end? What does one do for a seond act?

For some years prior to the event, I had given retirement quite a bit of serious thought. So, I continued to address my options.

Relaxation has never been a high priority with me. Those who can cease an active career and move to something like golf have my respect, but it is not a real option for me.

Something in or allied with academia had earlier appealed to me, but I began to have doubts as to whether my personality makeup would fit there. However, an opportunity to try it on an experimental basis came up.

During my year at the National Defense College in Kingston, Ontario, I became familiar with Queen's University in the same small city. In fact, in 1991, I was a featured speaker at the University's 150th Anniversary celebration. A friend from Defense College days, an Air Force general, was now on the staff of the Queen's business school. He arranged for an interview that resulted in my being named the executive-in-residence at the business school for the 1993-1994 academic year. This was a system in which a recently retired businessperson gave lectures, consulted with faculty members and students, and took part in activities such as seminars. The arrangement was always for one academic year, after which another candidate would be chosen.

My feeling about the experience was mixed. I was very positive about sharing insights into business in the classroom. The majority of the MBA students had worked for several years. Many were at the university under the auspices of their employers. As such, they were mature and often very savvy about business in general. Their favorite topics were business ethics and how it is possible to manage an organization as huge as Exxon.

What troubled me a bit was that the general atmosphere was overlain with political correctness and I found this difficult to accommodate. In the search for toleration of diversity, there seemed to be one type of diversity that was unpopular, and this was for ideas that differed from the party line or that would require significant change. However the experience was by and large a positive one and I am glad to have had it.

When I began to look around again, my attention was caught by the International Executive Service Corps (IESC), whose headquarters office was then in Stamford, Connecticut, adjoining the town of New Canaan where I live. It is the United States' largest private volunteer organization supplying Third World nations and emerging democracies with aid to small and medium private-sector businesses. The organization accomplishes this by placing American volunteers in U.S. foreign aid programs. Over the forty or so years of its existence, IESC had obtained some notably successful results. It was attractive to me because the aid went directly to small businesses rather than to local bureaucracies where the chances of its reaching the actual participants in the local economy severely diminished.

Although the CEO offered me an executive position, I wanted to try it out first. So, we agreed that initially, I would work on a strategic outlook for the organization as a volunteer in the headquarters' office. As I did this I found I liked the organization and its people, so I became executive vice president and worked at this from 1994 to 1997. By that time, I felt I had contributed what I could, so I relinquished the job and accepted a nomination to its board of directors, a position I had to vacate this year when I became seventy-six years old.

My time there as a volunteer and as a paid employee was certainly different from what I had known. For instance, my compensation during my employee period was approximately seven percent of what I had earned in my final years at Exxon, but I was not doing this for the money.

Rather than being steeped in a well-known corporate culture or ethos, IESC people come from a very diverse mix of training and background. Professionals in foreign aid come directly from university or from other foreign aid groups like the Peace Corps. The volunteers in the headquarters and in the field also come from very diverse backgrounds, and include individuals ranging from ex-CEOs of corporations to professional specialists. The glue that holds the organization together is basically altruism and a sense of doing something that counts.

This experience opened a whole new world to me in realizing that volunteer organizations can accomplish things that are difficult or impossible for government or for-profit business.

There were several personal highlights for me. One was engineering a stewardship system by which the organization could demonstrate its accomplishments to its major source of funds, the United States Agency for International Development (USAID). Other like organizations could only demonstrate what they had done. We could now demonstrate not only what we had done, but also how well we had done it by showing the results in terms of payout for effort extended. It made both the IESC and USAID "look good."

In my Exxon career I had been to many Third World countries and thus had a first-hand feeling for how much even a slightly improved economy can mean to citizens. That experience had also given me a feeling that foreign aid that goes to major projects often does little for the general population. Thus, the mission of the International Executive Service Corps, teaching business practices and technology to small private businesses, appealed to me as something that would achieve better lives for the recipient country's citizens.

Another highlight concerned Morocco, which at the time was a major recipient of U.S. aid to its private sector. In the US headquarters we began to get disturbing messages from our financial officer in Casablanca about the integrity of use of company funds. If we were disturbed, USAID was even more so, as they should have been, since they had entrusted the funds to us.

The employees in our Moroccan group, both Americans and Moroccan nationals, were upset because it was possible that under Moroccan law they could be accessories to whatever had happened.

All this naturally caused a lot of excitement in the Stamford headquarters where we were trying to bring the situation under control. I came up with the idea that I should take up temporary residence in Casablanca to supervise the operation and try to get everything straightened out. I had the idea that both USAID and the Moroccan employees would take a positive view of the executive vice president taking on an interim role there. Certainly it would demonstrate seriousness of purpose.

Thus, I began to live in a hotel in Casablanca and showed up at the office each day. I spent a lot of time in the USAID Moroccan headquarters in the country's capital at Rabat. I visited with worried clients. And I found out on behalf of the employees that they were not, in fact, accessories. In about six weeks, the situation was brought under control and we took steps to ensure that no recurrence would take place.

The whole episode was a small adventure for me that I enjoyed. Part of the enjoyment came from the fact that the events involved demanded spontaneous reaction and did not allow time for careful planning. I had to live by my wits, without the backup I had become used to in my primary career, and it was exhilarating.

It was even possible to take note of some colorful aspects of life in Casablanca, at five million people the biggest city in Africa after Cairo. For instance, most taxis were big Mercedes. Why so in a very poor country? Because an illegal ring had a shipping facility in Trieste to which European thieves would bring the hot cars. The ring apparently paid the thieves a small fraction of the cars' North African market price and then sold them in Casablanca and other centers for a hefty profit, even if the prices were much below those of legal sales.

And from there it was back to a relatively mundane existence in the headquarters.

It was during the time I spent with IESC that I decided to become a United States citizen. My reasoning had nothing to do with taxation, cost of living or any other economic factor; nor did it have anything to do with the more common reasons of religious or political freedom that have attracted immigrants over the years. When I first became familiar with Fairfield County, Connecticut, in my first headquarters assignment in 1977, I found it to be a place I liked more than any other in which I had lived. When Exxon moved its headquarters to Dallas in the late 1980s, I had only three years left until mandatory retirement. So, I kept my house in New Canaan because I wanted to retire there, and that is what I did.

Since I had decided to make New Canaan my home for good, it seemed that the only proper thing to do was to become a citizen. I took the oath of allegiance in a courtroom in Bridgeport, Connecticut, on November 18, 1994. I was quite moved by the speech the presiding judge made on that occasion. She had read over the list of those becoming citizens, and noted that many came from nations where there was no freedom of expression and other political freedoms. She entreated all of us to take part in American political life, at least to the degree of being knowledgeable, and above all to vote. All told, a very appropriate speech in my view.

Also, since retirement from my principal career, I have served as a consultant to a small oil and gas exploration and production company headquartered in Dallas, Texas. As with other retirement activities, it is a case where I got to a point that I felt I had contributed most of what I could. My hand was beginning to tremble as I received my fee. Thus what had been regular monthly visits to Dallas are now very few and irregular.

An interest during 2001-2003 was enrollment at the graduate school of applied psychology at a university near my home. I had long been puzzled by many aspects of human behavior and decided to exercise my curiosity in this regard. I was told that I would find human psychology as logical as mathematics and chemistry if I learned a new vocabulary and adopted different means of measurement, and so far this has proved to be true. I studied personality theories, psychological development over human lifetimes, and psychopathology. Additionally I undertook independent study to complete two monographs, one on the difference between religion and spirituality, another on the psychology of terrorists and the terrorized. I have found this education to be a profoundly enlightening experience, one from which I could have gained a lot of benefit much earlier in life.

For five years, I have written sporadic op-ed pieces for the weekly newspaper in the town where I live, *The New Canaan Advertiser*. These usually concern energy or business issues, and less often are political or attempt to be funny. I collect rejection slips from some of the most prestigious publications in the nation. Lately I have been writing a book. So, Act II has consisted of many things. As I get older, I may try golf.

Trying to Be an Author

When I set out to write a book, the degree of my naïveté would be difficult to exaggerate. It would have been beyond my comprehension if someone had suggested that I would write ten drafts before I got even close to being satisfied. For the first five or so of these, as draft followed draft, each was an absolutely different book from the preceding one, while the last five have been fine tuning. Looking at the first five, the entire theme and purpose of each was different from the one that preceded it. One draft was about the thrill of discovery of ideas and things. Another was about the role that curiosity plays in our lives. Yet another mixed a description of the oil and gas exploration and production business with the adventures I had in that business. You get the picture. The truth that I ultimately had to face is that I did not know what I wanted to write about. I realized that the main theme of what I wanted to write about is the adventures and insights that were offered up by a combination of my education, my work career, and my sense of curiosity.

Then there came the matter of my writing style coming under the critical eye of my family, a person in the book publishing business, and a professor who teaches university-level style and composition. The message had several components. One was that as a teller of stories I was good, but when I departed from this I was not so good. Another was that I wrote like a scientist and documented every point. The message here was, "You don't have to document everything. We will believe you. But find a way to tell a story that grabs the reader rather than documenting and instructing."

Each of these suggestions was well-based and had merit. But the best advice of all was, "Develop a style and then stick with it. Start every new phase with something that immediately gets the reader's interest and attention rather than developing it gradually. Keep your book to one theme, the stories of your experience. Read at least something from the works of the great writers of memoirs."

I have been an avid reader since early in elementary school days. Many times, I have found myself captivated by writing skill, particularly the ability to write in such a way as to stimulate my neurons into making me feel that I am right there with the characters in a novel, or writing that gives me a sudden burst of understanding of something that has been difficult to comprehend. Thus, it is strange that such reading never translated itself into the ability to allow me to emulate it in writing.

I have read that some writers are meticulously careful as they write each sentence and even each word. My habit is quite different. I think hard about something I want to write and then set it all down rapidly in words. Then I begin the process of attempting to give it style, untangling sentences, searching for exactly the correct word or phrase to clearly express a thought.

But in the end, what allowed me to feel comfortable with what I had written was to keep telling myself to think of the advice I had been given and to revise, revise, revise, and revise again until what I read back to myself communicated most easily and pleasingly.

And by those processes, the book you are reading was created.

You Can Go Back Again
A La Recherche Du Temps Perdu

One day, after I thought I had finished writing this book, I was reading a new biography that covers the lives of two men who are on my list of American heroes, Ulysses S. Grant and Mark Twain. The biography is *Grant and Twain*, by Mark Perry (8).

In an attempt to research a book he had long intended to write about the Mississippi River (and which ultimately became *Life on the Mississippi*), in 1882 Twain traveled down the Mississippi from St. Louis to New Orleans and all the way back upstream to Minneapolis. The author makes clear that in addition to being research for the book, the journey would be an attempt by Twain to relive the glory days of his young manhood as a riverboat pilot that he relished so much in memory. I too had relished those days vicariously when as a young man I read *Life on the Mississippi*. In particular, he caught my imagination by writing in that book that Mississippi river boat pilots lived an idyllic existence because they were extremely well paid and were totally their own bosses, beholden to no man. I read and reread the passages about how his mentor, Mr. Bixby, taught him the trade, because I was fascinated by how the learning experience took place with Bixby alternately being a friendly bully and then daring Twain by giving him sole responsibility for the ship during night watches on treacherous stretches of the river.

As regards to his late-life trip on the Mississippi, the biography reads, on pages 98 and 99, "Twain was irrepressible, talking to pilots, gamblers, river men, clerks, war veterans and engineers and meticulously following his own progress on navigation charts. He was joined on the river by his old mentor and friend, Horace Bixby, the riverboat pilot. 'Sam was ever making notes in his memorandum book, just as he always did,' Bixby remembered."

And further, "One day later, Twain's appetite for piloting was finally satisfied by Lem Gray, the Gold Dust's captain. 'When we got down below Cairo, and there was a big, full river—-for it was high-water season and there was no danger of the boat hitting anything so long as she kept in the river—-I had her most of the time on his watch. He would lie down and sleep, and leave me there to dream that the years had not slipped away; that there had been no war, no mining days, no literary adventures; that I was still a pilot, happy and care-free as I had been twenty years before.'"

That passage certainly spoke to me, because something like that has happened to me many times as I grow older. Sometimes I have sought to make it happen, as when I went back at age seventy to fields in Alberta where I had hunted ducks and geese and upland birds forty five years earlier, as I described in the tale titled *Landscapes*. On many more occasions it happened when I was still at work for Exxon, and I would be reviewing oil and gas prospects with young earth scientists and petroleum engineers. On those occasions, I would sometimes feel the same excitement I had felt when I was their age, when it would be evident that "It really counts to do something that counts." Or I would repeat with them the type of earlier experience I'd had when my curiosity drove me to figure out something that had puzzled me and I suddenly saw the answer.

On yet other occasions, it happens when I am speaking with my adult offspring and we reminisce about long ago incidents in our lives, and sometimes we begin to see things in the remembered events that escaped us years ago as they happened.

I think the folk wisdom that "you can't go back again" really means that it is impossible to shift one's current life back into the ambience of long-ago times, no matter how much one yearns for that. However, it is very possible to relive the some of the greatness of earlier times by placing oneself in similar circumstances or by association with younger persons who are living similar experiences now.

We seek to relive painful parts of our pasts in attempts to deal with them rationally. However, there can be life-affirming experiences in mentally recreating positive times from long ago. In some ways, you can go back again. Is that not what I am doing by writing this book?

It is one of the privileges of growing old.

Afterword

This book has been structured around the telling of tales of life experiences concerning people, places and issues over the span of a seventy-six year lifetime. The earlier ones reflect a very naïve young man's view of the world. As time progressed, I was given a magnificent opportunity to absorb a steadily widening and a deepening span of experience. Throughout all the experiences related in the tales, my sense of curiosity made me question and explore what I was witnessing.

It seems appropriate and fitting at this point to think about whether there are common threads that are woven into and among the experiences, and if there are, whether there is meaning that can be taken from them.

One recurring idea is that we fulfill ourselves to a greater degree under adversity and challenge than we do under comfort and ease. Most of my thinking on this subject has been covered in the tale titled, "Why Do We Perform Better Under Adversity?" One particular experience that served to convince me that we do so is covered in that tale. I refer to the case in which the threat of failure in betting a company's future entirely on a single heavy oil project produced a far superior way to achieve the same thing with minimal risk to shareholders. That experience and many others have led me to conclude that the human brain is programmed to function more effectively when anxiety is present. Stephen Jay Gould's reaction to being diagnosed as having a terrible form of cancer is a vivid example, as described in the tale, "Dealing with Risk."

This same thought is the message of Newberg and D'Aquilli quoted in "Why Do We Perform Better in Adversity?" This miracle may be the product of anxiety-produced chemical stimulation of the brain, but that is only a surmise on my part. Adrenalin or some other stimulant may not only increase our physical functionality, but may also heighten our mental awareness and functionality.

I must admit that the evidence for this is mainly empirical (other than what has been quoted from Newberg and D'Aquilli) and is based largely on my personal experience. However, *Bartlett's Familiar Quotations* has twenty-two listings under the word "adversity," illustrating what others have thought about it. The closest to the point I have been describing is from Sir Francis Bacon (English, 1561-1626): "Prosperity doth best discover vice, but adversity doth best discover virtue." It does seem evident that human beings are far more prone to doing stupid and careless things when easy times supply little stimulation to do the magnificently clever things that anxiety can promote. This idea is almost sure to offend and disturb some personalities. What about the "happily ever after" that we all seek and strive to obtain? It does present a conundrum.

In the type of experience I have covered, challenge and anxiety have given me a sense of being alive that I miss when they are not present, and a sense of well-being and contentment when they have stimulated me to do something that has been rewarding to others and to me. No doubt, variations in our individual neurological makeup, which I know can be due to both nature and nurture, equip individuals differently in this regard.

The second truism that my life experiences have caused me to repeatedly consider has to do with the bond among human beings. Each of us is responsible for his or her own behavior, including our behavior in matters concerning others. What I am thinking about here is well expressed by Dr. Nancy Andreason in her recent book, *Brave New Brain* (1). Dr. Andreason is Chair of Psychiatry at Iowa State College of Medicine. The quote is pretty highfalutin' language, but it does exactly express what I think is true:

"Although we cannot easily demonstrate its existence by scientific methods, we all have a sense of self. We rightly see ourselves as unique individuals, moral executors who are confronted with decisions that we freely choose to make, and linked by those choices to a bond with other people in a community that we call human society. As far as we know, only human beings have this sense of self that permits us to both act as free moral agents and also to stand outside ourselves and appraise our thoughts and actions as 'right' or 'wrong.' There are many different words for this sense of self: soul, spirit, conscience, and consciousness. Whatever we call it, as human beings we recognize the dual existence of both our individual identity and of an inexplicable force that transcends individuals and reflects the collective bond that we all have as living beings. This sense of individual self and a union with other human beings in our present, past, and future is the impetus behind selflessness, humility, compassion and sacrifice."

And further, "If we want to prove the existence of the moral reality that also transcends individuals and links them to one another, we will learn more by looking at exemplary human lives. The recognition that each of us has an individual identity that we call a self or a soul, that our self is guided by a moral imperative, and that the moral imperative also transcends our individual self and links us to other human beings exists with indelible certainty across all cultures and continents. It is no coincidence that Jesus and Confucius independently came up with the 'Golden Rule.'"

This certainly captures what I think I learned from life experience. I seemed to understand it at various points in my life and then let it lapse again and present a need to be reintroduced. Clearly, the experience I had as a seventeen-year-old working in a gold mine, described earlier in "A Seventeen Year Old Learns the Reality of Work," showed me that I had to be an integral part of a work team both for my own benefit and for the benefit of my co-workers. We depended on each other.

I needed to be reminded again when I was successful as an individual contributor early in my earth science career. I scorned executives until I got a jolt that made me realize that their real function is to optimize the benefits of interdependence. I had made an immature and arrogant judgment of them.

Adam Smith recognized this issue in *The Wealth of Nations*, when he wrote that society progresses by dividing labor into coordinated specialties. During my span of life, I have been reminded again and again of how dependent we are on one another and how much that cooperation enriches our lives. A functional family is all about the bonds among people that allow them to support one another, and this is equally true in work groups and other human organizations. A symphony orchestra is a wonderful example of a large group being effective only when their independent efforts are totally coordinated. Healthy competition brings out our best efforts, but it functions very productively in an interdependent group. I am very conscious that what I learned in this regard simply echoes and confirms for me personally an age-old theme that has been described by countless others, notably by John Donne:

"No man is an island, entire of itself; every man is a piece of the continent, a part of the main."

A third theme that is woven into most or perhaps all of the tales I have told and the insights I have described is curiosity. I have related that my mother told me that when I was a small boy, my nickname in my large extended family was Donny Why, and that my sense of curiosity often taxed the patience of my relatives.

It has never been completely clear to me why some people have a strong sense of curiosity. Is it genetic, the result of neurological makeup? Is it a learned behavior, dependent on nurturing? As is often concluded about questions of this sort, it is probably due to a neurological predisposition that gets noticed and encouraged. What seems clear is that a sense of curiosity can be both a strong asset in dealing with life's issues as well as a source of enjoyment. Curiosity about things, issues, situations, and emotions leads to learning and being involved. It is probably a requisite for creativity.

In *The Golden Thread* (6), Bruce Meyer points out that our nature is based on change, and that we are in a continual state of learning something new, discovering something different, and adapting our understanding of the world on a daily basis.

And further, I found this nugget in Mihaly Csikszentmihaly's *Creativity* (3): "Practically every individual who has made a significant contribution to a domain remembers a feeling of awe about the mysteries of life and has rich anecdotes to tell about efforts to solve them."

As we educate ourselves over our lifetimes in an attempt to make sense of the world around us, we are influenced by what we read, see and hear from those that society has deemed to have something to contribute to our understanding. Like us, they were curious and simply tried to comprehend the meaning of their own lives and the lives of others.

Introspection makes me believe that my own life was strongly enriched by the fact that curiosity drove me to some rare and wonderful destinations, both geographic and cognitive, as suggested by the title I chose for this book. With those observations, I come to the end of the stories I wanted to tell.

Don McIvor, New Canaan, Connecticut, October 14, 2004.

Seventeen Year Old Gold Miner, 1945

International Nickel Field Crew, Northern Manitoba, 1948

Duck Hunting With My Boss, Peace River, Alberta

Crossing the Catumbela River, Angola

Digging a Land Rover out of a drainage canal, Angola

At the startup of the first heavy oil production module,
Cold Lake, Alberta, 1985.

Caves with 1,000 year old Christian Frescoes,
Xinjiang, China

The Lost City, near Kashgar,
Xinjiang, China

The Curator of The Lost City,
Xinjiang, China

A Uygar Gentleman,
Xinjiang, China

Looking at the tracks of a Pterodactyl in the Himalayas,
Xinjiang, China

Director and Senior Vice President, Exxon, 1985

Bibliography

(1) Andreason, Nancy: *Brave New Brain*, 2001. Oxford University Press, 198 Madison Avenue, New York, New York.

(2) Constantin, Peter, (Editor): *The Undiscovered Chekhov, Forty Three New Stories*, 1998, Seven Stories Press, 140 Watts Street, New York, New York.

(3) Csikszentmihaly, Mihaly: *Creativity*, 1996, Harper & Collins, 10 E 53rd Street, New York, New York.

(4) Gould, Stephen Jay, *Full House*, 1996, Harmony Books, New York, New York.

(5) Hermann, Arthur, *How the Scots Invented the Modern World*, 2001, Three Rivers Press, New York, New York.

(6) Meyer, Bruce, *The Golden Thread*, 2000, Harper & Collins Publishers Ltd., 55 Avenue Road, Toronto, Ontario.

(7) Newberg, Andrew, & D'Aquilli, Eugene: *Why God Won't Go Away: Brain Science and the Biology of Belief*, 1998, Ballantine Books Division of Random House, Inc., New York, New York.

(8) Perry, Mark, *Grant and Twain*, 2004, Random House, New York, New York.

(9)Petroski, Henry, *To Engineer Is Human: The Role Of Failure In Design*, 1992, Vintage Books, New York, New York.

(10)Rees, Sir Martin, *Just Six Numbers*, 2000, Basic Books, New York, New York.

(11)Yergin, Daniel, *The Prize: The Epic Quest for Oil, Money, and Power*, Simon and Schuster, 1230 Avenue of the Americas, New York, New York.

"This is a wonderful little book which I thoroughly enjoyed. Don McIvor has had a full and wonderful life and his book describes the fun he had along the way to becoming a wise and thoughtful business leader."

John C. Whitehead
Chairman, The Lower Manhattan Development Corporation and former Deputy Secretary of State

"While not an autobiography, Don McIvor's selection of events and observations reflect a lifelong intellectual curiosity which had the benefit of an early beginning in modest circumstances on the Canadian Prairie. The reader will quickly perceive the writer's intensive interest in 'exploration' but well beyond finding oil and gas, the subject of his geological career. A life well lived and successful by any measure."

Allan R. Taylor
Retired CEO, The Royal Bank of Canada

"There was never a question which Don McIvor did not investigate for an adequate answer. He has always been a passionately curious man...He not only has a superior intellect, but also the intellectual integrity to clearly state facts without spin. No one ever accused him of being a bore or a hypocrite. I never knew him to have prejudices of any kind, except for the fact that he does not suffer fools gladly. His perennial pursuit was the right answer to a question, the truth."

"His story should be read by young men and women to realize that if they believe in themselves, pursue excellence, and maintain moral integrity, they more likely will realize their human potential."

Hobart C. Gardiner
Former President & CEO,
International Executive Service Corps.

"An excellent job of story telling, a hard enough task, but you succeeded at making the themes of those stories relevant and universal, and that's even harder. You did some serious thinking about who you are and what that self-knowledge means. All in all, a fine job!"

Rod McQueen
Former news anchor,
Canadian Broadcasting Corporation

— *Grindstone Press* —

Grindstone Press **QUICK ORDER FORM**

Fax orders: 877-733-0528 Send this form.

Telephone Orders: Call 877-733-0528 toll free or 323-972-2923

E-Mail Orders: wittyfools@gmail.com

Postal Orders: GRINDSTONE PRESS, @Witty Fools Productions, PO Box 481058, Los Angeles, CA 90048, USA. Phone 877-733-0528.

Please send more FREE information on:
❒ Other Books ❒ Speaking/Seminars ❒ Consulting ❒ Blogs

Name ______________________________

Address ______________________________

City ______________ State __________ ZIP ____________

Telephone ______________________________

E-Mail Address ______________________________

Shipping

US: $2.00 for first book and $1.00 for each additional book.

Canada: $4.00 for first book and $2.00 for each additional book.

Payment: ❒ Check ❒ Credit Card ❒ VISA ❒ Master Card

Card Number: ______________________________

Name on Card: ______________________ Exp. Date ________